# THE
# STOIC LEADER

First published in Great Britain in 2025 by
Michael O'Mara Books Limited
9 Lion Yard
Tremadoc Road
London SW4 7NQ

EU representative:
Authorised Rep Compliance Ltd
Ground Floor, 71 Baggot Street Lower
Dublin D02 P593
Ireland

Copyright © John Sellars and Justin Stead 2025

All rights reserved. You may not copy, store, distribute, transmit, reproduce or otherwise make available this publication (or any part of it) in any form, or by any means (electronic, digital, optical, mechanical, photocopying, recording, machine readable, text/data mining or otherwise), without the prior written permission of the publisher. Any person who does any unauthorized act in relation to this publication may be liable to criminal prosecution and civil claims for damages.

A CIP catalogue record for this book is available from the British Library.

This product is made of material from well-managed, FSC®-certified forests and other controlled sources. The manufacturing processes conform to the environmental regulations of the country of origin.

For further information see
www.mombooks.com/about/sustainability-climate-focus

Report any safety issues to product.safety@mombooks.com and see
www.mombooks.com/contact/product-safety

UK edition:
ISBN: 978-1-78929-830-7 in paperback print format
ISBN: 978-1-78929-878-9 in ebook format
US edition:
ISBN: 978-1-78929-891-8 in paperback print format
ISBN: 978-1-78929-931-1 in ebook format

1 2 3 4 5 6 7 8 9 10

Cover design by Julyan Bayes
Typeset by Barbara Ward
Printed and bound by CPI Group (UK) Ltd, Croydon, CR0 4YY

www.mombooks.com

# THE STOIC LEADER

## Ancient Lessons to Succeed in Business

JOHN SELLARS
*and* JUSTIN STEAD

Michael O'Mara Books Limited

**To everyone who has contributed to and supported the Aurelius Foundation**

For the love of my daughters – Sofia, Valentina and Carolina – that these pages may guide you when I no longer can, in all that life will bring. And to my wife, Natalia, whose joy, love and forgiveness saved me from myself.

*Justin Stead*

# CONTENTS

| | |
|---|---|
| Introduction | 7 |
| Chapter 1: Meeting the Ancient Stoics | 13 |
| Chapter 2: A CEO Meets the Stoics | 25 |
| Chapter 3: The Stoics on Control | 35 |
| Chapter 4: Understanding Control | 49 |
| Chapter 5: What Is Character? | 59 |
| Chapter 6: Building Integrity as a Leader | 69 |
| Chapter 7: Social Animals | 83 |
| Chapter 8: Stoic Teamwork in Business | 91 |
| Chapter 9: Facing Challenges | 103 |
| Chapter 10: The Journey to Become a Stoic Leader | 113 |
| Chapter 11: Stoic Decision-Making | 127 |
| Chapter 12: Meditations on Decision-Making | 141 |
| Chapter 13: Reflecting on Time | 159 |
| Chapter 14: Stoic CEO Time Management | 171 |
| Chapter 15: The Big Picture | 185 |
| Chapter 16: A Strategic View from Above | 195 |
| Chapter 17: Next Steps | 205 |
| Chapter 18: Daily Stoic Disciplines | 213 |
| Chapter 19: Final Reflections | 223 |
| Further Reading | 235 |
| Acknowledgements | 241 |
| Endnotes | 247 |
| Index | 252 |

# INTRODUCTION

The American business executive and one-time US presidential candidate Steve Forbes described the *Meditations*, a collection of personal writings by Stoic philosopher and Roman Emperor Marcus Aurelius, as 'a must-read for business leaders'.[1] The former US President Bill Clinton once said that the *Meditations* was one of his favourite books.[2] Earlier, in the eighteenth century, Prussian Emperor Frederick the Great described Marcus as 'my hero, my model'.[3] It makes sense that people in positions of power and leadership might be drawn to read works by famous leaders of the past, but the striking feature of Marcus Aurelius' *Meditations* is that it says very little directly about how to be a great leader. There are no insights into how he ran the Roman world. What we find instead are deeply personal reflections about how to cope with the ups and downs of life and how to be a good person – reflections drawing on the wisdom and insights of Stoic philosophy. Marcus' own response to the question of how to be a good leader was simply to be a Stoic. This did not mean to be 'stoical' in the common English sense of the term; instead, it meant to follow the teachings of the ancient Greek school of Stoicism.

Other Stoic philosophers *did* reflect directly on what it meant to be a good leader. The Roman Stoic Musonius Rufus, when visited by a king from Syria, declared that it was vital for anyone in such a leadership position to study philosophy – specifically Stoic philosophy.[4] Musonius argued that a good leader must develop what the Stoics called the four cardinal virtues of justice, moderation, courage and wisdom. A leader's role involves making sure the country, organization or company they direct flourishes and that the people within it do too. But, Musonius asks, how can anyone achieve that if they don't know what's genuinely good or bad? A good leader should treat people within and outside their organization fairly – they need to be just, so they need to understand what justice is. They need to exercise self-control when making decisions – the virtue of temperance or moderation. Sometimes, they will need to make difficult decisions, and this will require courage. Most vital of all, they will need to develop skill in decision-making, becoming an expert in making calm, rational and informed choices. This is the virtue of prudence or wisdom.

In this book, we will introduce you to the core ideas of Stoicism and show how they can be put into practice in the context of business leadership. We will draw on our different experiences to do so – John has spent the past couple of decades as an academic, reading, writing and teaching Stoic ideas; Justin has spent decades as a successful CEO, and now chair, of multiple companies, benefitting from Stoic ideas throughout his journey. Chapters alternate between the two of us and are paired around a series of key topics. First, you'll learn about ancient Stoic ideas, then you'll see how they can be put into practice in a business setting. We'll reflect on individual Stoics along the way, especially Marcus Aurelius, drawing on examples of how Stoic ideas were used in the ancient world. We don't see these ancient figures as perfect role models to be emulated but instead as flawed human beings just like us, who were doing their best to navigate the challenges of their personal

— INTRODUCTION —

and professional lives. We don't think these two things can be neatly separated – it's never 'just business' – and so the journey to become a better leader is also the journey to become a better human being. What task could be more important?

## Chapter 1

# MEETING THE ANCIENT STOICS

## JOHN SELLARS

> *We Stoics are not subjects of a despot;*
> *each of us lays claim to his own freedom.*
>
> Seneca, *Letters* 33.4

# Principal Stoics

**Zeno** – son of a businessman in Cyprus, the founder of Stoicism

**Cleanthes** – second head of the Stoa, formerly a boxer who worked a night shift watering gardens so he could philosophize during the day

**Chrysippus** – third head of the Stoa, originally from Turkey, a formidable intellect and important logician

**Diogenes of Babylon** – an immigrant from the Middle East who would go on to become head of the Stoa

**Antipater** – from Tarsus in modern-day Turkey, he would also become head of the Stoa

— MEETING THE ANCIENT STOICS —

**Panaetius** – from the Greek island of Rhodes, an associate of the famous Roman general Scipio Africanus

**Seneca** – leading Roman Stoic, originally from Spain, tutor to the young Nero and later his adviser

**Musonius Rufus** – Roman Stoic actively engaged in politics who taught in Rome

**Epictetus** – slave from Turkey who gained his freedom, attended the lectures of Musonius and founded his own school of philosophy in Greece

**Hierocles** – Stoic writer active in the first centuries AD, author of *Elements of Ethics*

**Marcus Aurelius** – Roman Emperor and author of the *Meditations*

There is no such thing as Stoicism, only Stoics. This is so in two ways. First, the philosophy of Stoicism flourished for some 500 years in antiquity and each of the major figures interpreted the core ideas in their own way, dropping elements that they found less convincing and adapting them in light of their own circumstances and life experience. There is no single, authoritative source that definitively states what Stoicism is. Second, although the ancient Stoics developed complex theories on a huge range of topics, from cosmology and meteorology to logic and grammar, for them and many other ancient thinkers, philosophy was fundamentally about how to live. It was something to be put into practice in your own life. As one of the most notable Stoics, Seneca, commented, philosophy isn't – or shouldn't be – about complex word games but instead 'it moulds and constructs the soul, it orders our life, guides our conduct, shows us what we should do and what we should leave undone'.[5] The goal is to live a Stoic life; to become a Stoic.

## Marcus Aurelius

Marcus Aurelius is probably the most famous Stoic, and the *Meditations* is without doubt the most widely read Stoic text today. Marcus was of course not only a philosopher but also Roman Emperor, and so leader of the Western world. He was not born into this role, but it came to him through a series of complicated twists and turns. It began with the death of his father when Marcus was just three years old. He was adopted and brought up by his grandfather, and other members of the extended family guided him. When Marcus was a young man, Emperor Hadrian, in search of an heir, decided to adopt Antoninus Pius but stipulated that Antoninus should himself adopt the young Marcus. This set Marcus on the path to become emperor.

Marcus gained a reputation for being a just and fair ruler, although modern commentators have inevitably questioned some of his actions. As emperor, he engaged in wars and defended the borders of the Empire when they were under threat. The final years of his life were largely spent on campaign in central Europe, defending the northern border of the Empire from the incursions of local Germanic tribes. *Meditations* was probably written during this period, while he was leading the Roman army on the front line. There is a comment in the book noting that at least part of it was written while he was at Carnuntum, a Roman base not far from modern-day Vienna, the site of which can be visited today.

## MEDITATIONS

*Meditations* was probably never written to be widely read. It is a series of notebooks in which Marcus Aurelius reflects on a wide range of topics, from his own mortality to dealing with other people. There's a good deal of repetition as he reflects on the same issues again and again. There are also quotations from other works he was reading at the time. It gives us a privileged window into his thought processes and some of the challenges that he faced as emperor. The title *Meditations* is modern; the recorded Greek title translates as 'To himself'. Marcus probably did not add a title; these were just his private notebooks.

## Epictetus

Marcus tells us that one of his teachers gave him a copy of the *Discourses* of the Stoic philosopher Epictetus, and it is clear that this work was an important influence on his thinking. On the face of it, Marcus and Epictetus could not have been more different. Marcus was emperor, drawn from the highest circles of Roman society, while Epictetus was a slave from Asia Minor, without money or power, taken to Rome against his will, eventually granted his freedom after decades in bondage and soon after leaving Italy to start a philosophy school in western Greece. The *Discourses* as we have them are presented as lecture notes based on discussions in his school, written down by one of his pupils.

Epictetus does not seem to have had much interest in politics or business, although many of his students probably came from wealthy Roman families and were destined for careers in those fields. His repeated lesson to them was that before they were in any position to govern, they ought first learn to govern themselves.

Many of the central themes in Epictetus' *Discourses* can also be found in the work of another Stoic teacher who had been active in Rome, Musonius Rufus. We are told that Epictetus attended Musonius' lectures, perhaps when he was still a slave. The records we have of Musonius' lectures show a focus on highly practical, everyday questions about marriage, educating children, what to wear, how to decorate your home and how to cut your hair. Musonius was also active in Roman politics: he was closely associated with a group of Senators – sometimes referred to as 'the Stoic opposition' – who tried to overthrow the Emperor Nero, and his principled behaviour based on his Stoic values led to his banishment. Musonius' philosophy was a highly practical guide to how to live, and it greatly influenced Epictetus.

## DISCOURSES AND HANDBOOK

We usually credit Epictetus with two works, the *Discourses* and the *Handbook*. In fact, he didn't write either of them. The *Discourses* were written by one of his pupils, Arrian, who would go on to become a noted historian and have a career as a political and military leader. This work records conversations that took place in Epictetus' classroom at his philosophy school in Nicopolis in western Greece. The four books of the *Discourses* we have today are probably only half of what Arrian wrote down. The much shorter *Handbook* was also compiled by Arrian, pulling out key ideas from the *Discourses* to form a portable summary of Epictetus' philosophy. In the Middle Ages, it was adapted and used to train monks.

## Seneca

Another famous Roman Stoic is Lucius Annaeus Seneca. Like his contemporary Musonius, Seneca was a highly practical thinker, drawing on Stoic ideas to navigate the dramatic ups and downs of his life. Originally from Spain, Seneca operated at the highest levels of Roman politics, where a dispute with Emperor Caligula almost cost him his life. Later, he was sent into exile by the Emperor Claudius, probably for political reasons, on perhaps fictitious charges of adultery. It was during his exile on the island of Corsica that Seneca wrote a number of his early works. He was eventually recalled to Rome, on the condition that he take on the role of tutor to a young boy in the imperial family: Nero. When Nero went on to become emperor, Seneca found himself at the very heart of Roman power, acting as his adviser. Also a successful businessman, Seneca became one of the wealthiest people in Rome. Yet, as Nero became more suspicious of those around him, Seneca found himself in a highly dangerous situation. Withdrawal from public life was not an option; walking away would have looked like a rejection of Nero. As a plot to remove Nero from power developed, Seneca was accused of being involved and Nero ultimately ordered him to take his own life.

### DIALOGUES, LETTERS AND MORE

Seneca wrote a series of short essays on topics such as how to live a happy life, how to manage anger, the importance of leisure and the shortness of life. These are known as the *Dialogues*. Two much longer essays deal with topics closely connected to politics: *On Clemency* and *On Benefits*. Later in life, Seneca wrote a series of letters to his friend Lucilius, called the *Moral Letters*. Something of a polymath, Seneca also wrote about topics in physics in his *Natural Questions* and produced a series of tragedies. Taken together, Seneca's works form the largest body of Stoic writing to survive from antiquity.

## Stoics in Athens

All the Stoics mentioned so far were active in the first two centuries AD, under the Roman Empire. Stoicism as a philosophy was already centuries old by this point, having been founded much earlier in Athens, the spiritual home of ancient philosophy. The most famous of all the Greek philosophers, Socrates, lived in Athens in the fifth century BC and was tried and executed in 399 BC, on charges of corrupting the youth. Socrates would go on to become a role model for many later thinkers, including the Stoics. Epictetus once famously said, 'If you are not already a Socrates you ought to live trying to become a Socrates.'[6] In the century that followed, Plato and Aristotle lived and taught in Athens, at the Academy and the Lyceum. At some point around 30 BC, the philosopher Zeno of Citium started teaching at the Painted Stoa, a covered colonnade on the northern edge of the central marketplace in Athens. His followers came to be known as 'Stoics' – the people who gather at the Stoa.

According to the biographical tradition, Zeno had been travelling by boat to Athens from his home in Cyprus on a business trip for his father when his ship was wrecked. He managed to make it to shore, although his cargo was lost. As he recovered from the ordeal, he started to browse a bookstall nearby. There, he started reading an account of the philosophical conversations of Socrates written by the philosopher-soldier Xenophon. Zeno was impressed by what he read. He asked the bookseller where he could find someone like Socrates and, at that moment, a philosopher called Crates walked past and the bookseller said, 'Follow that man.'[7]

Zeno followed Crates for a while and then spent time studying at Plato's Academy. Ultimately, he had no desire to be merely a disciple of someone else and so started teaching in his own voice. He quickly attracted an audience, one of whom, Cleanthes, is said to have worked all evening watering the gardens in Athens so he could be free to listen to Zeno during the day.[8] After Zeno died, Cleanthes took over as head of this new philosophical school, the Stoa. He was in turn succeeded by Chrysippus, an astute logician who also wrote at length about the nature and treatment of emotional disturbances. It is often said that Chrysippus was the most important of these early Athenian Stoics and that he did much to systematize and organize Stoic thought. Once established, the Stoic school flourished in Athens until about the middle of the first century BC. Among later Athenian Stoics, the most notable are Panaetius of Rhodes and Antipater from Tarsus, whose ideas we will come back to in later chapters.

***

As we can see, the Stoics were a cosmopolitan group, coming from right across the ancient Mediterranean world and from all strata of society – aristocrats and slaves, emperors and immigrants – all united by a shared set of beliefs and values. This was completely in accord with Stoic thinking, which argues that we ought to think of all humankind as members of a single global community, united by our shared rationality.

Chapter 2

# A CEO MEETS THE STOICS

## JUSTIN STEAD

> *To be like the rock that the waves keep crashing over. It stands unmoved and the raging of the sea falls still around it.*
>
> Marcus Aurelius, *Meditations* 4.49

Traditionally, when people look at Marcus Aurelius and Seneca they view them both as enlightened Stoics. My first philosophical impressions were the same, but as my business career developed I started to see them in a broader light. They were conflicted individuals – desperate to be living deeply as Stoics but compelled to compete and fulfil their significant responsibilities as leading men of Rome in a time of continual military conflict, expansion and external threat, all within a ruthless political environment that was as cut-throat as any power forum that has ever existed. As soon as one donned the purple, he placed a target on himself and those around him.

Neither Marcus nor Seneca were perhaps business orientated in their first calling, but they had to be business and economically astute in the execution of their public and professional duties; Marcus and Seneca were essentially senior business executives within their daily roles. Therefore, let us think of Marcus as both chairman of the board and CEO during a high-functioning period of the Roman Empire in the second century, while considering Seneca as chief operating officer within a completely dysfunctional Roman corporation.

## Marcus Aurelius: CEO of the Roman corporation

Marcus Aurelius is perhaps best known for the *Meditations*, which offer profound insights into Stoic philosophy and self-governance. However, his responsibilities extended far beyond penning philosophical reflections; Marcus governed an expansive empire fraught with challenges, overseeing complex economic systems, military campaigns and public welfare initiatives.

He is an outlier in history and did not become emperor through traditional means, such as a military conquest, a civil war or a bloody coup. He just happened to be living in an extraordinary period of Roman history, the second century, when a series of controlled and careful transitions of power transpired – from Nerva to Trajan, Trajan to Hadrian, Hadrian to Antoninus Pius, and Antoninus Pius to Marcus. Considering the times, these were all very well-managed power transitions where the 'best candidate' was handed the reigns of the imperial juggernaut.

In his role as chairman and CEO of the Roman Empire, Marcus faced pressures that would make even the most seasoned executive tremble. He was not only responsible for the welfare of millions but was also required to ensure the functioning of a vast economy that relied on trade, agriculture and taxation. The Stoic cardinal virtues he espoused – wisdom, temperance, justice and courage – were not abstract ideas but necessary tools for survival in a tumultuous political environment. They were his daily toolkit for better executive decision-making, although he likely had to compromise these values at times because of his imperial duties – I can picture Marcus cringing at the cost and unnecessary loss of life in the incredibly popular gladiatorial games in the Colosseum.

Unfortunately, we may never see the likes of Marcus Aurelius in a seat of such power again. Even within modern democracies, the dynamics and mechanisms of getting into power have changed so radically – think Donald Trump – that it may be difficult for us to imagine someone with a profound, deep and reflective character like Marcus Aurelius breaking through unless there was a complete catastrophe like a third world war. Society would have to come to its knees and realize that a different, higher moral leadership would be required to lift us from the ashes. For example, Nelson Mandela rose to lead South Africa in response to the abhorrent apartheid system – a time when people needed a higher moral calling to lead them to a better place for *all* people.

## Seneca: Chief operating officer of the Roman corporation

Seneca is perhaps better understood from a leadership perspective as Rome's chief operating officer, navigating the treacherous waters of court politics and his own vast economic interests during the turbulent reign of Emperor Nero. A renowned Stoic philosopher and adviser, Seneca's influence extended beyond philosophy; based on his vast wealth, we can assume he was a shrewd and sophisticated businessman, experienced in financial planning, forecasting and lending. He is well known for his lending practices, which were at times on the 'sharp end' of doing business. Excluding the emperor, he was the richest man in Rome.

He bounced in and out of favour for years and was exiled by Emperor Claudius for a decade before being called back to Rome to tutor the young Nero. As COO of Rome in Nero's court, Seneca had to manage the CEO's wishes and directions carefully, a delicate and shrewd process of personal and business management in itself.

As one of the most eloquent voices of Stoicism, Seneca's works – such as his *Moral Letters* and *On the Shortness of Life* – provide keen insights into personal ethics and leadership. His adeptness in the 'boardroom' and his understanding of the business landscape, during a period when the Roman economy was frequently challenged, are especially noteworthy. Seneca's ability to blend philosophical contemplation with practical action allowed him to effectively advise Nero, for a period, despite the complexities of managing an emperor known for his unhinged emotional outbursts, volatility and unpredictability.

## Deeply committed Stoics conflicted as leaders and businesspeople

In the modern business landscape, ethical decision-making and strong moral leadership are more important than ever, especially in the public markets. We continually see employees and shareholders defrauded by unethical leadership – think Elizabeth Holmes and the Theranos scandal or Sam Bankman-Fried and the bankruptcy of FTX. Cases like these show that it is vital to turn to the timeless wisdom of ancient philosophies amid the often chaotic interplay of profit motives, competitive pressures and the allure of rapid success. The teachings of Marcus Aurelius and Seneca resonate deeply with today's leaders, providing essential lessons on how to be a successful, ethical CEO.

Marcus Aurelius and Seneca were not simply philosophers cloistered in the ivory tower of theoretical intellect. They were practical leaders, engaged in the complexities of governance, commerce and finance. Their lives provide a unique vantage point from which to explore the intersection of Stoic philosophy and business management. As we delve into their philosophies, we will elucidate the significant impact they had not only on the ethical frameworks we explore today but also on the practical mechanics of managing large enterprises.

## Leadership in the storm

As we draw comparisons between Marcus and Seneca, we shall explore their approaches to leadership and the pressures they faced as they navigated complicated governance. Both exemplified characteristics essential for any successful business leader today:

1. **Ethical decision-making:** Both leaders utilized Stoicism as a guide for making tough decisions. While Marcus' reflections often focused on inner strength and humility, Seneca emphasized the importance of ethical behaviour in commerce. Both understood that leadership required balancing personal integrity with systemic pressures, advocating for decisions grounded in moral authority. They wanted Rome to be a good corporate citizen.

2. **Civic responsibility:** As civic leaders, they both adopted policies that reflected a deep concern for their constituents, demonstrating the Stoic belief in the common good. Marcus regularly deliberated on policies that benefitted public welfare, while Seneca used his influence to promote economic stability during times of crisis. By leading responsibly, CEOs can act in the best interest of employees, financial partners and the delivery of sound ESG strategies (Environmental, Social, Governance).

3. **Management of resources:** The complexity of managing vast resources during their reigns is comparable to the modern resources leaders must manage. From logistics to human capital, their experiences offer a useful guide to overseeing extensive operations and making strategic decisions under pressure. Strong financial management utilizing smart cashflow, profit and loss, and balance sheet awareness were essential for both Marcus and Seneca.

4. **Navigating adversity:** Each faced formidable challenges; Marcus dealt with external threats to the Empire, and Seneca manoeuvred through the perils of court life under a volatile ruler. Their ability to maintain a level-headed Stoic composure amid turmoil showcases their leadership resilience. Like any good CEO or COO, they were continually updating a SWOT matrix (strengths, weaknesses, opportunities, threats) and risk analysis

across the entire Roman Empire. They had to act swiftly and accurately when trouble arose, focusing their time, energy and resources where it counted. A good example of this would be Marcus spending so much time along the Danube holding back the enemies of Rome – as CEO, he felt it was his duty to be there on location.

5. **Mentorship and influence:** Both leaders took on mentorship roles, imparting their wisdom to their advisers and the next generation. No doubt both men considered the sharing of their Stoic principles important, and their legacies extend beyond their lives through the students and followers they inspired.

## Stoicism as a blueprint for modern business

In examining the roles of Marcus Aurelius and Seneca, we unveil a unique model of leadership that is both philosophical and practical. As we explore their insights throughout this book, we shall discover how their thoughts on moral authority, ethical leadership and strategic decision-making are applicable to the contemporary corporate world.

By bridging the gap between Stoicism and practical business applications, this book will illuminate how leaders today can learn from these great Stoics to build a successful business that harmonizes profit with integrity, fostering enduring success that transcends the bottom line. With the wisdom of the ancient Stoics guiding our steps, we can strive to better define our own professional paths with clarity and purpose in the high-stakes environment of modern business.

## Summary & Reflection

- Marcus Aurelius and Seneca were not simply ancient philosophical icons but executive leaders operating in the harsh realities of the Roman Empire. Their Stoicism was not theoretical – it was a leadership model.

- Marcus embodied the CEO archetype – wrestling with duty, personal virtue and macroeconomic pressures. Seneca, the COO, balanced ethics and political survival in a dysfunctional regime.

- Both men remind us that Stoic leadership is not about perfection but persistence. Their legacies offer CEOs a potential leadership blueprint: ethical clarity, emotional control, strategic patience and, above all, moral courage in the face of volatility.

- As we move deeper into this book, their stories serve as a clarion call: being a Stoic in business is not just about managing outcomes but mastering oneself.

Chapter 3

# THE STOICS ON CONTROL

## JOHN SELLARS

> *Things outside my understanding are nothing at all in regard to my understanding. Master this, and you stand upright.*
>
> Marcus Aurelius, *Meditations* 7.2

As a leader, it might seem natural to expect to be in control of many things. One of the first lessons the ancient Stoics teach is that in fact we control very little of the world around us. The opening lines of the *Handbook* of Epictetus state:

> *Some things are up to us and some are not up to us. Up to us are our opinions, desires, choices, aversions, and – in a word – everything that is our own action. Not up to us are our bodies, property, reputation, job, and – in a word – everything that is not our own action.*
>
> Epictetus, *Handbook* 1.1

Epictetus goes on to add that our own actions are always free and unhindered but all the things that are not our own actions – our bodies, money, job, reputation – are by nature weak, enslaved and subject to outside control. This is stark and uncompromising. Much of what we ordinarily think we control, in fact we do not, Epictetus insists. All that we can really control are our own thoughts and beliefs. Everything else is, as he puts it, 'not up to us'. And yet, most of us spend a lot of our time pursuing or worrying about things that fall into this second category.

For Epictetus, the key to living a happy life is understanding this distinction and – more importantly – not mis-categorizing things:

> *If you think that what is naturally slavish is free, and what is not your own is your own, then you will be obstructed, you will grieve, you will be disturbed, and you will blame everyone. However, if you only think what truly is your own to be your own, and what is not your own not to be yours, then no one will ever be able to control you, no one will be able to obstruct you, you won't blame anyone or find fault with anyone, you will do nothing against your will and have no enemies; no one will be able to harm you because no harm can ever touch you.*
>
> Epictetus, *Handbook* 1.3

As he puts it in the *Discourses*, if you don't care whether the tyrant cuts your head off or not, there's nothing the tyrant can do to coerce you.[9] That is of course an extreme example, but the general principle can be applied in a wide range of situations: the more we are attached to particular things or outcomes, the more upset we'll be if we lose those things or if events don't go our way. Epictetus' point is that *by definition* external things and events are never fully within our control, so if we tie our happiness to them then we'll quite literally make ourselves hostages to fortune. While many people might think that this is just an inevitable state of affairs, Epictetus insists that it is a *choice* we make. If we tie our happiness to things that are 'not up to us', then our happiness will not be up to us either.

If this sounds like a clever philosopher talking in theory with no realistic sense of how it would work in practice, it is worth remembering that for a good part of his life Epictetus was a slave, with little control over the external aspects of his own life. Happily, most of us have no idea of what that would really be like, but in those extreme circumstances, Epictetus likely knew all too well what was, and was not, within his control. He knew what could be taken from him, but he also knew what *no one* could take from him.

Epictetus presents this as a blunt and stark contrast in order to jolt us out of our usual ways of thinking. In practice, we can do much to try to influence things that are not up to us. We can take care of our bodies, even if we cannot guarantee whether they will get sick or injured; we can strive towards goals, even if we can't completely ensure that we'll be successful. Just because we can't fully control the outcome doesn't mean that we should give up and do nothing. But if we want to avoid living a life full of frustration and disappointment, then we must keep in mind this key Stoic insight: the only things we fully control are our own actions – our judgements, beliefs and choices.

If that sounds like we don't control very much, Epictetus reduces it even further. Our beliefs and choices are ultimately the product of the value judgements we make. If I judge that something is good or useful or beautiful, then I'll believe that it is something worth having and I'll choose to try to get it. My choices and desires will be the product of my value judgements. Epictetus summed up this idea in a famous phrase:

> *It is not things that upset people, but their judgements about things.*
>
> Epictetus, *Handbook* 5

Whatever happens to us, whether we find it upsetting or not, depends on the value judgements we make. We know this because sometimes we see people react in quite different ways to the same situation, some remaining calm and largely indifferent, while others are noticeably disturbed. Of course, there are some extreme events where *everyone* seems distressed. But most of our lives are occupied with more mundane events which may or may not be disturbing, depending on the judgements people make. This idea, stated by Epictetus, inspired Albert Ellis and others to develop cognitive behavioural therapies in the twentieth century.[10] Stoic thinking about control is not merely a historical curiosity but in fact the foundation of a good deal of modern psychotherapy.

## The angry brother

One of the many things we don't control – and one that can often cause us a lot of frustration – is other people. We don't control what they do, say or think. This is the inevitable flip side of the fact that no one can control what *we* do, say or think. It goes both ways. One striking example of this is recounted in Epictetus' *Discourses*. A man came to visit him one day, upset at the fact that his brother was angry with him. 'How', the man asked, 'do I get my brother to stop being angry with me?' Epictetus said the following:

> *Philosophy does not claim to secure for people anything external. If it did, it would be trying to do something outside its domain.*
>
> Epictetus, *Discourses* 1.15.2

Slightly exasperated, the man repeated his question, 'But how do I get my brother to stop being angry?' Epictetus replied:

> *Bring him to me and I will tell him. But I have nothing to say to you about his anger.*
>
> Epictetus, *Discourses* 1.15.5

The lesson is simple: the man cannot control his brother's anger, and the only person who can do anything about that is the brother himself. What the man *can* do is attend to *his own* response to his brother's anger. We cannot control the emotions of other people, but we can control our *reactions* to them. As we have seen, what we control is the judgement *we* make about it, which in turn shapes our own emotional response. Rather than focus too much on how other people behave – something 'not up to us' – we should instead focus our attention on *our* judgements about what other people do, for this is the element over which we have control.

## Antipater on archery

Not only do we not control other people, we don't even control the outcome of our own actions. We might decide what we *want* to do, but not whether or not we are successful. The Stoic philosopher Antipater, who taught at the Stoa in Athens, illustrated this with the following analogy:

> *Take the case of one whose task it is to shoot a spear or arrow straight at some target. One's ultimate aim is to do all in one's power to shoot straight, and the same applies with our ultimate goal. In this kind of example, it is to shoot straight that one must do all one can; nonetheless, it is to do all one can to accomplish the task that is really the ultimate aim.*[11]
>
> From Cicero, *On Ends* 3.22.

The thought behind this example goes like this: the archer shooting the arrow can never *guarantee* that he'll hit the target, because once the arrow has been shot other things might interfere with it hitting the target, such as an unexpected gust of wind. The same applies to the captain of a ship who, no matter how skilled and accomplished he is, cannot guarantee that he'll get to the harbour safely because he has no control over the weather. Similarly, a doctor, no matter how expert she may be, cannot guarantee that she will be able to save all of her patients – there are just too many variables that might impact the outcome. In all these cases, Antipater suggests that the appropriate thing to do is to focus not on the outcome but on *doing the best one can* to reach the outcome. The doctor's goal should not be to save all of her patients – which would be setting herself up for failure, distress and disappointment – but instead the more realistic and attainable goal of *doing all she can* to help her patients. For the archer, the goal is not to hit the target, something out of his control, but to shoot as straight as he can. Hitting the target is something 'preferred' – we still want it to happen, but it is not our immediate goal. Rather than focusing on the outcome, we should instead direct our attention to the activity, to developing the appropriate skills so that we can perform the activity as best as possible. And of course, the more we develop those skills the more likely we are to hit the target or save the patient, even if those outcomes can never be guaranteed.

Antipater used this example in an analogy. The point he wanted to make is that we ought to think of *all* that we do along the lines of the archer. What matters most is not the outcome, which we don't control, but what we *do*. When thinking about ethics, we might say that what matters most is having good intentions. In life in general, what matters most is doing the best we can, feeling confident that we did not let ourselves down due to lack of effort or integrity; this is more important than how things actually turn out. Even in the worst situations, if we can walk away confident that we acted as best we could, we can hopefully avoid overwhelming feelings of disappointment. We did not hit the target on this occasion, but at least we did all we could to shoot straight.

In his book *Busy: How to Thrive in a World of Too Much*, Tony Crabbe suggests that we ought to give up on the idea of ever being fully in control and instead replace it with the idea of mastery.[12] With all of the information and the demands that assault us in modern life, it is now more or less impossible to ever be fully on top of everything and to feel in control. The risk is that we constantly feel that we are drowning.

Crabbe proposes that we simply give up on the unrealistic ambition of trying to be completely in control and instead direct our efforts to developing mastery of the key skills that we need in our roles. Rather than feeling like we are drowning in information and demands, this will give us a renewed sense of agency by focusing – in the language of Epictetus – on what is 'up to us' rather than what is not. Although he makes no mention of Stoicism, Crabbe's advice for managing the often overwhelming demands of modern life echoes that of the Stoics: focus on what you can control, developing your own skills and mastery, not on what you can't, the final result.

## Diary of an ancient CEO

Epictetus spent much of his life as a slave, all too conscious of how little of his own life he controlled. One of his most devoted readers – the Emperor Marcus Aurelius – lived at the other end of the social spectrum, with all the freedoms and privileges that the ancient world could offer. The *Meditations* was originally written as a private diary or notebook, recording his reflections on life at the top. While at first glance it might seem that Marcus had far more freedom and power than Epictetus, the pressures of his role as emperor made it difficult for him to maintain a sense of control in the face of the countless competing demands coming at him from all sides. The emperor needed the guidance of the slave.

Among the many things that Marcus reminds himself he cannot control are other people and what they do, what others think of him, his posthumous reputation, his physical health (which was often not good) and how long he would live. Left to his own devices, it seems fairly clear that Marcus would have preferred to have lived a life of quiet scholarly study; he was by temperament an intellectual and had spent many years in his youth studying philosophy with some of the leading Stoics of his day. But circumstances had conspired to make him emperor, and he felt it was his duty to embrace that role and do it to the best of his ability. Marcus wrote his reflections while on campaign fighting against Germanic tribes in central Europe. There was no way he could guarantee how the conflict would turn out, or the fate of the Roman Empire that had been entrusted to him; all he could do was focus on his own judgements, choices and actions. In the *Meditations*, he continually reminds himself of this fact. His list of things he cannot control includes:

- All external events and states of affairs.
- His own body, which can get sick or damaged of its own accord.
- Anything in his mind that is not its own activity.
- Anything in the past, which, by definition, cannot be changed.
- Anything in the future, which, at the present moment, does not exist.

What does that leave him? The only thing that Marcus – the most powerful man in the Western world – thinks he really controls are his own actions in the present moment.[13] 'What can I do here and now?' And as we have seen with the archery analogy, what one can do here and now is *aim* to achieve something, not guarantee success. Any time and energy spent worrying about the outcome will merely take mental resources away from acting the best one can.

While this might seem like an extremely limited sphere of control, Marcus also stresses a positive aspect to this. Like all other Stoics, Marcus thinks that the key to living a good, happy life involves the cultivation of the right frame of mind, an excellent character. We'll come back to this in Chapter 5. The key point for now is that our character shapes and is shaped by our judgements and actions. What we do in the here and now – the one thing under our control – determines how well we live, regardless of the outcome. So although we control seemingly very little, what we do control is fundamental to our wellbeing. If the only thing that is genuinely good is acting well, and the only thing genuinely bad is acting poorly, then we have complete control over what is good and bad in our lives.[14] Everything else – success or failure, unexpected events, what other people say and do – will inevitably impact us in various ways, but none of it is inherently good or bad. We have *complete control* over what really matters.

As emperor, Marcus probably spent quite a lot of time feeling out of control, all too conscious of the problems he could not fix, the wars he could not escape, the crises that could not be avoided. The fact that he reflects on these topics in the *Meditations* suggests these were things with which he struggled. His response is to remind himself that, despite all the outside noise and the challenges constantly facing him, the one thing that matters most remains completely within his control. No matter how chaotic things might seem, no one can take that away from him.

Chapter 4

# UNDERSTANDING CONTROL

## JUSTIN STEAD

> *You have power over your mind – not outside events. Realize this, and you will find strength.*
>
> Marcus Aurelius, *Meditations* 8.47

Understanding control can significantly enhance a CEO's decision-making ability, ultimately leading to more effective leadership and organizational success. The most pertinent aspect of this crucial Stoic concept is the misunderstanding of how much control a CEO actually has as the leader of a business. In my experience, there are so many more factors out of my control versus in my control. I did not realize this until I landed in my first CEO role at the age of thirty-nine.

I had the mistaken understanding that a CEO could wave their magic executive-control wand and problems would be made good. During my years observing how some of the best retail and brand CEOs in the world operate, I often looked at them only through the narrow lens of the power they could wield, not through what they actually influenced.

## Understanding the dichotomy of control as a CEO

1. **What's within our control or influence:** These are aspects of our lives, actions and decisions that we have the power to influence. For a CEO, this includes how they respond to challenges, the strategic vision they set for the company,

their leadership style and the organizational culture they endeavour to establish.

2. **What's outside our control or influence:** These are external factors beyond our influence, such as market conditions, competitor actions, regulatory changes and even the opinions and behaviours of stakeholders. While we can prepare for and respond to these factors, we cannot directly control them.

---

You will notice that alongside things in or outside our control, I have included things we can *influence*. I have done this because often it is not as binary as either 'I have control' or 'I do not have control' – the office of the CEO can influence a situation rather than control it, and still achieve outcomes.

I made mistakes as a young CEO, thinking that if I spoke long enough or directly enough – or very occasionally, loud enough – I could control an outcome. How did I come to realize that these were mistakes? Yes, the results fell short of the business requirements that I wanted to achieve, but more importantly, I could sense I was not winning the team over to me or to the cultural transformation we needed to make to be successful. People were not buying in – yet!

What I realized over the ensuing months and years, and especially as the senior leadership team around me grew close, was that exerting influence from a distance was more powerful as a CEO than trying to control a potential outcome directly. By taking a step back and not trying to solve every problem personally, I created space for teams to explore issues in greater detail and discuss further. This resulted in better communication and collaboration to solve problems, with teams buying into the overall company strategy rather than simply searching for my confirmation as the CEO.

A great example of this in action is the historical development of the e-commerce and digital channels that are the backbone of most retail brands in the world today. From the late 1990s onwards, every retailer or brand in the world wanted to efficiently grow their e-commerce business. This strategy was coupled with continuing to invest in physical locations around the world. However, the capital expenditure requirements would not allow for every planned new store to be opened alongside the continual infrastructure and marketing investment for e-commerce. Decisions had to be made, considering budgetary and finite capital resources, around how many stores could be opened within a particular year, how much money could be spent on physical retail expansion versus the building up of the medium- and long-term e-commerce channel.

During these discussions within my business, I often left teams to debate the physical store locations versus long-term e-commerce growth, versus the budget requirements for that year, without my involvement. There were millions of pounds of capital expenditure to deploy within the budget, tied to a strategy with clear return-on-investment objectives. By encouraging more debate and not dictating from the top, teams put forward fascinating creative solutions. I recall one situation where an original £2 million capital expenditure project for a full upgrade to a significant London location was reduced to less than £500,000 for a lighter touch improvement, and the remaining balance was allocated to the digital growth strategy and other e-commerce projects.

I had the executive control to spend the £2 million, but by refraining from the desire to control everything, the CEO's *influence* helped us to arrive at a more effective solution than I may have reached simply by exerting control throughout the process.

## The role of the dichotomy of control in improving decision-making for CEOs

1. **Enhanced focus on actionable areas:** By recognizing the limits of control, CEOs can redirect their focus towards actions and decisions that are within their purview. This clarity helps eliminate wasted time and energy on external factors they cannot change, leading to more productive strategic planning and execution.

2. **Reduced anxiety and stress:** Understanding what is and isn't in their control allows CEOs to cultivate resilience in the face of uncertainty. When faced with challenges or crises, focusing on controllable elements can mitigate stress and anxiety, enabling clearer, more rational decision-making under pressure.

3. **Empowered leadership:** A CEO who embraces the dichotomy of control fosters an environment of empowerment within their organization. By encouraging team members to take ownership of their responsibilities – focusing on what *they* can control – they promote a culture of accountability, initiative and innovation, which can lead to better overall performance.

4. **Strategic risk management:** By acknowledging the uncertainties in their environment, leaders can develop robust risk management strategies. Rather than attempting to control external factors, CEOs can prepare contingencies and adaptive strategies that account for various scenarios, increasing organizational resilience.

5. **Improved stakeholder communication:** Understanding the dichotomy of control helps CEOs to communicate effectively with stakeholders. By framing discussions around what can realistically be controlled versus what cannot, a CEO can set appropriate expectations, build trust and foster transparency regarding decision-making processes and outcomes.

6. **Long-term vision:** The dichotomy of control encourages a long-term perspective. By focusing on values, mission and strategic goals – elements within their control – CEOs can lead their organizations with purpose. This long-term vision guides day-to-day decisions and inspires their teams, even as external circumstances fluctuate.

The dichotomy of control is a powerful tool for CEOs, sharpening their decision-making ability and ultimately enhancing organizational effectiveness. By distinguishing between what they can influence and what they cannot, leaders can become more focused, resilient and strategic to secure their organizations' futures in an unpredictable market landscape. Embracing this concept not only elevates individual leadership capabilities but also cultivates a healthier, more proactive organizational culture. Indirect influence is equally as important as control from the 'Office of the CEO', if one is wielding the executive power carefully, within a well-articulated and clear strategy across any organization.

As I read the *Meditations* every morning, and have done so for decades, I have the distinct impression that Marcus Aurelius, even as the supreme ruler of the Roman Empire, spent a lot of his time in silence, reflecting on and noticing his own moods and emotions. He was also clearly a keen observer of others, situations and potential outcomes. He knew his control was finite but his influence perhaps wider – and he wielded his power more effectively as a result.

UNDERSTANDING CONTROL

## Summary & Reflection

▶ The role of a CEO is not to be an all-powerful commander but a discerning strategist – one who must know the boundary between influence and control. True leadership doesn't come from micromanaging outcomes but from empowering teams and creating clarity in the chaos.

▶ Influence can yield better results than direct intervention by giving teams the power and freedom to discover creative solutions independently. Knowing the difference between what you can control and what you can influence offers clarity and purpose. The dichotomy of control does not weaken the authority of the leader; it strengthens their position in the business.

## Chapter 5

# WHAT IS CHARACTER?

## JOHN SELLARS

> *Perfection of character possesses this: to live each day as if the last, to be neither feverish nor apathetic, and not to act a part.*
>
> Marcus Aurelius, *Meditations* 7.69

Imagine a brick sitting on a flat surface. You push it with your finger. It is quite heavy, so you have to use some force. The brick moves for as long as you apply pressure but, as soon as you take your finger away, it stops. Now imagine a ball of the same weight on the same surface. You push it with the same degree of force and it starts moving. Unlike the brick, it moves quite easily and – this is the key difference – it keeps moving even after you have stopped pushing it; it rolls on its own.

What's the difference between the brick and the ball? Why do they respond differently to the same external force? The answer is, of course, obvious: they have different shapes. The shape of the object determines how it responds to the external forces with which it comes into contact.

The Stoics used analogies like this to think about the role of character.[15] The world assaults us with a dizzying array of external forces, and how we respond to them is determined by our character. Imagine three quite different people faced with a dangerous situation. One might be too nervous to do anything and just freeze. The second might unthinkingly throw themselves into it, risking themselves and perhaps others, while the third might bravely but cautiously face the situation head-on. In the traditional language of virtues, we would describe these three people as cowardly, reckless and courageous. The important point is that how they behave is determined not by the *situation*, which is the same for all of them, but by their *character*.

When we think about character in this sense, what we have in mind is a person's beliefs and values, their personality and their habitual ways of thinking and acting. These things are all closely inter-related. We have already seen Epictetus insist that all we really control are our value judgements. Those judgements determine what we think ('this is good'), which in turn determines what we do ('I'm going to try to get this good thing'). If we perform the same action repeatedly, we will start to develop a habit, and at its core, our character is simply a collection of habitual ways of behaving. Change your judgements and you can change your habits; change your habits and you can change your life.

## Good character

Character determines how we respond to the situations in which we find ourselves. Someone prone to anger – that is, someone with a habit of judging that it is a terrible thing when events don't go their way – has a certain type of character: one that the Stoics would judge to be bad. Why? Two reasons: first, such a person is no longer able to make calm, rational decisions, and second, they have made a mistake about where true good and bad reside. We have already seen the Stoics claim that true good and bad reside within us, in our judgements and actions, but what reasons did they give for this view?

Drawing on ideas first developed by Socrates, the Stoics argued along the following lines.[16] External things such as wealth or physical strength, which most people judge to be inherently good, are not so, because they can be used in both good and bad ways. While one person who wins the lottery might share their winnings among friends and family members in need, another might descend into a self-destructive spiral of excessive partying and alcoholism. A physically strong person could use their presence either to intimidate those weaker than themselves or to protect them from other threats. In both cases, what the person does with their money or strength comes not from the external thing but from their character, which determines how they use it. If someone has a self-destructive, addictive personality, winning a large amount of money could turn out to be the worst thing that could happen to them.

## The virtues

So, character is key. It determines how we behave, how we respond to external situations and how we make use of external things. Someone with a bad character will never be able to live a good, happy life, no matter how externally successful they might seem to be. But what precisely do we mean when we say 'good character'? The Stoics described it with reference to a series of virtues. The term 'virtue' might seem outdated today, and it is not a word we hear very often. The Greek word behind this, ἀρετή (*arete*), has connotations of something being excellent or admirable. To be virtuous is to be a good example of something. Even today we might describe a new product or gadget as having many virtues. The Stoics often talk about someone being virtuous, by which they mean being a good, admirable person, but they also talk about individual virtues that they thought always come together in a package – you can't have one without the others. The four central virtues are justice, courage, moderation (or self-control) and wisdom (or prudence). These are the character traits they believed were the defining features of a good person.

Like 'virtue', the terms 'courage' and 'justice' can sound very grand and perhaps a little intimidating. Who would claim to embody these things today? But there is no reason to feel intimidated, and the core ideas are ones to which we can all relate. To say that someone is 'just', is simply to say that they treat other people fairly. While courage might sound like something reserved for battlefields, people can display courage in a wide range of everyday situations, such as when someone feels fear or nervousness about doing the right thing but does it anyway. Moderation or self-control is more straightforward but, as we all know, sometimes difficult to master. Prudence is simply the ability to make good decisions, carefully assessing situations rather than acting impulsively and without proper attention to the consequences. Epictetus says that it is always clear which sorts of people we admire: no one praises a cheat, a coward, someone with no self-control or someone who keeps making bad decisions.[17] Even if we have never thought of it in these terms before, implicitly most of us probably already admire the four core Stoic virtues.

## The benefits of virtue

In this sense we can say that someone who has these virtues is admirable. But what are the benefits of being virtuous? Does being a good, admirable person conflict with doing what's best for us? Is there a tension between doing the right thing and acting in our self-interest? These were questions that the Stoics tackled directly.

Earlier in this chapter, we noted that external things that most people tend to think of as good – like money, status, health and strength – are not inherently good because they can be used for both good and bad ends.

When it comes to the virtues, the Stoics argue that we are dealing with something that *is* inherently good precisely because it *always* benefits us. The person with money who is just, moderate and prudent knows how to use it effectively and so can benefit from their wealth. But, the Stoics argue, the same applies to someone without much money. They will also benefit from being just, moderate and prudent as they navigate the challenges of getting by on limited means. In other words, no matter what the circumstances might be, the virtues are *always* worth having. That's what makes them good.

The next question the Stoics will ask is: where is your self-interest? Is it in pursuing external things like wealth and status, or is it in developing a good character? It should be fairly clear by now what their answer is. If a good character always benefits us, but external things can potentially harm us if we use them badly, then obviously we ought to prioritize character development over the pursuit of external success.

Character will sustain us through difficult times and will enable us to effectively manage and enjoy success in the good times. Wherever we are in life, we need good character.

## Pursuing external success

This might make it sound as if the Stoics are largely indifferent to external success in life. Epictetus often says things that add to that impression, such as his account of what we do and don't control. He can seem to be saying that we ought to focus just on what we can control – our thoughts and judgements – and pay no attention to everything else. That's a misleading impression, though, and the Stoics thought that it was entirely natural for people to pursue all the external things that enable us to survive and to enjoy a successful life. We are all born with a natural survival instinct, and we do what we must to get food, water, shelter and all the other things we need in order to live. We look after our health and provide for our families out of similar natural instincts. All this is normal and proper, they insist. A person who completely neglects their own wellbeing – indifferent to their health, perhaps depressed, with no concern for their future – we might consider as not functioning properly; something has gone wrong.

So, the Stoics insist that it is entirely natural for us to pursue success, wealth, good health and all the other external things that add value to a good life. In their language, these things are always 'preferred' over their opposites. No one would actively choose to be sick or to struggle to secure the basic needs of life. But – and this is the key point – these things are *never* as important as a good, virtuous character. As we have seen, without that we may not even benefit from all these external things if we manage to get them. Character always comes first.

This leads the Stoics to warn that we should never compromise our character in the pursuit of external success or money. To do that would be to destroy the one thing we need if we are to appreciate and benefit from whatever success we have.

## Virtue is its own reward

When Seneca was advising the young Nero, he tried to teach him the value of acting virtuously. Doing the right thing should never be done with the thought that some benefit might come from it further down the line. It should be done purely for its own sake, because it is the right thing to do.

*The true profit of virtuous actions lies in the doing, and there is no fitting reward for the virtues apart from the virtues themselves.*

Seneca, *On Clemency* 1.1.1

Similarly, if we do someone a favour or give them a gift, Seneca advises that we shouldn't expect anything in return. What matters is the action of helping someone out and the joy that it brings to both us and them. If they are able to help us out at some point in the future, that is obviously welcome, but it should never be seen as a repayment. We should not think of people who we help to be in any way in our debt, and we should make that clear. The size of the gift or the extent of the support is not important either; what matters is the good intention to help someone else, without thought of getting anything in return.

But this is not a case of pure altruism. The Stoics think we *do* benefit in this situation; indeed, they think we *really* benefit. By performing these virtuous actions – for the right reason, with no thought of material reward or payback – we develop and consolidate our virtuous character, the one thing that is genuinely good and truly benefits us. And of course, 'good begets good', as the saying goes. The person who treats other people fairly and respectfully will, over time, develop a reputation for doing just that and, as a consequence, be seen as the sort of person with whom others will want to work and do business. The employer who gains a reputation for treating their staff decently and equitably is unlikely to have a serious problem retaining and recruiting people. The minimal costs involved in 'doing the right thing' will be more than offset by other benefits down the line. However, as Seneca insists, you don't do it as part of some complex calculation; you do it because you know it's the right thing to do and you want to be the sort of person who does the right thing. In the process, you also lead by example.

## Chapter 6

# BUILDING INTEGRITY AS A LEADER

### JUSTIN STEAD

> *Waste no more time arguing what a good man should be. Be one.*
>
> Marcus Aurelius, *Meditations* 10.16

There is an old saying: 'There is no substitute for experience.' Another layer could be added to this statement: 'There is no substitute for experience and the building of character.'

In my reflection and the perspectives of the people I have worked alongside during my career, I have always maintained a commitment to honesty. This might seem like an unusual assertion, but we all recognize that people often say one thing while thinking another; or worse, they choose to deceive. In many business environments, this gap between words and intentions becomes especially pronounced, particularly in conversations between leadership and the CEO. Employees often say what they think the CEO wants to hear – not the reality of the situation the employee is dealing with or trying to accomplish.

It is a universally acknowledged truth among leaders that we often learn more from our failures than our successes. Personally, my setbacks have stung deeply, and it has taken time for me to learn and move forward effectively. These combined points of being honest and direct while still being ambitious and learning from mistakes is the journey not only to building a successful career but also great character.

One of my greatest mentors, Richard Gundy, the president of Fossil Group during its remarkable growth as a global accessories powerhouse, taught me invaluable lessons about character. When I worked under his guidance in 2003, overseeing the US business in addition to global Fossil watch sales, I witnessed first-hand the importance of character when confronted with a challenge.

## An early lesson in character

A particularly challenging situation arose with a major partner in the United States, regarding margin requirements after the holiday trading season – a notoriously tense period for brand–retailer relationships, during which retailers often wield more influence. I was expecting a difficult conversation with our most important retail partner because, after the season, we would not be contributing margin to our partner's results for the period. I meticulously prepared for this meeting, rehearsing my approach, and chose to fly to New York to discuss the issue in person.

Richard observed my preparation and asked about my plans. When I shared that I intended to meet the partner face-to-face, he simply replied, 'Come to my office and let's resolve this issue efficiently so we can all move on.' Following his lead, I entered his office, and within ten minutes the issue had been expertly addressed.

Richard called the partner, requested a few minutes of her time and, with clarity and confidence, explained our position. He allowed me to present the details, explaining the situation, and professionally concluded the call by expressing our anticipation for the next scheduled meeting.

I was inspired by Richard's composure and skill. He handled the situation with politeness, directness and rationality, allowing the partner to voice her thoughts, all while concluding without major conflict or rancour. The lessons which can be taken from this encounter were profound:

- **Respect is earned:** Maintaining respect is crucial to fostering open dialogue. You cannot convey important messages without it.

- **The value of honesty:** Senior management appreciates direct, honest communication that is effective and efficient.

- **Character is key:** Delivering tough messages is only possible through consistent character.

It was Richard's unwavering character that made the difference in that call. The partner respected Richard not just for his position but for his straightforwardness, integrity and long-term vision for the partnership.

Through this encounter, I learned that a short, impactful conversation can yield significant results. As I continued to advance in my career, I committed to embodying the Stoic characteristics of brevity, frankness and integrity – hallmarks of strong character.

## Why character matters in business

One of the most critical periods in my career came soon after my arrival in the United Kingdom from the United States in

2006. I thought I was moving up in the world, coming over to London to be the CEO of a substantial business as part of a well-orchestrated succession plan. The business was fatigued but had significant potential with new, dynamic shareholders.

As it turned out, the succession did not go as smoothly as planned – internal leadership and management turmoil meant I didn't immediately take full executive control of the business as CEO as originally outlined. It was a period of enormous pressure for everyone involved as more issues inevitably appeared across the business while the CEO transition was supposed to take place. Factions appeared, conflicts arose, unexpected behaviours were revealed.

The situation could have gone one of two ways: I would either be fired and returned to the United States, or I would take over the business as CEO as planned. I had two factors working in my favour. One, I was determined to do the right thing at any cost, no matter what the people around me might be doing. Second, I had unfailing support from my best friend, Joe Eastin, and all my key mentors from the past who steadied me throughout this period. There is no substitute for good character, but where is good character fostered? Through hard-won experience and outstanding mentorship. You are the measure of who you surround yourself with throughout your career.

During a three-month period in 2007, when all sorts of issues were being played out in the business, my inner circle of support kept my attention focused on my character – on being Stoic. For example, they helped me think through a scenario in which I lost everything. As a Stoic, once you have thought about the situation you are facing in this way, it is much easier to return to the arena of battle because 'death has been imagined' – and therefore processed and accepted.

This period of uncertainty at the business came to a head one Sunday, when I met the major shareholder and offered my resignation in the best interest of bringing closure. Unbeknownst to me, within the previous twenty-four hours the major shareholder had been unexpectedly challenged by outside parties related to the business.

What to do? It was surely straightforward, I assumed. I would be fired, exited from the UK and the business would continue on without me.

Fascinatingly, the exact opposite happened. The shareholder acted in a way that totally shocked me, telling me directly: 'You are not going anywhere!' In no uncertain terms, he reminded the outside parties of their responsibilities to the best interests of their constituents and shareholders, and told them Justin Stead would be taking over formally as CEO in short order, to take the business forward in *their* best interests – something that would be proven over time. This was a stunning decision in a very complicated and difficult business situation at the highest level, with hundreds of millions of pounds at stake and thousands of employees potentially impacted.

Meeting the shareholder later, I asked him about the reason for his decision to back me. He said that although most of the board supported me, it was primarily my *character* that had tipped the decision in my favour, both in how I had conducted myself during the process and how they saw me taking the business forward.

## The brown bag test

In any field, a person can train themselves over and over in their skill set for the chance to be successful in the heat of competition. The same principle applies in life through Stoic practice, but the key is to be ready to apply one's Stoic skills when one is most vulnerable or tempted to take short cuts. The higher one goes in life, including in business, the greater the stakes and risks become. Life often presents significant tests of character when one least expects it, and mine, early in my CEO career, arrived one fateful morning in London.

A key partner in the business, whose success was integral to our future, requested an unusual meeting. Instead of our usual coffee shop rendezvous, he met me in my office on Oxford Street in London. With small talk behind us, the atmosphere shifted dramatically when he placed a brown paper bag on the table. Curiosity turned to shock as I learned that the bag contained not coffee but a substantial sum of cash – wrapped £50 notes that could total between £50,000 and £100,000. The message was unmistakable: this was a bribe, an insurance policy meant to ensure that our partnership continued to prosper.

In that moment, silence enveloped us. It was an uncomfortable pause, heavy with the weight of moral choice. After regaining my composure, I gently pushed the bag back, asserting that I would not require such a thank-you. I politely but firmly insisted we forget the conversation. To my surprise, the partner accepted my rejection with calmness and moved the conversation forward as if nothing had happened. This choice, rooted in integrity, moderation and justice, laid the foundation for a successful partnership that would last years and culminate in a remarkable financial exit from the business for us both.

## The cosmic character record

As Stoics, we believe that we come into this world with nothing and that, ultimately, we depart with nothing. All we seem to possess is just on loan – our money, our belongings, our relationships. Therefore, the only enduring treasure that is worth keeping and accumulating is the greatness of our character. Our true wealth lies in the cosmic record of our actions – shaped by our intentions and derived from our character.

So, did the money in that brown bag tempt me? Yes, of course. At the time I was cash poor, my savings and other assets were intertwined with significant personal and business debts. Yet, I recognized that succumbing to such temptation would contradict the very essence of my responsibilities to my team and stakeholders, and, most importantly, it would have damaged my character.

## Decision-making through good habits and mentorship

The choice to reject the bribe aligned with my commitment to integrity and justice, but this was reinforced by my chairman,

Don McCarthy. Don was a remarkable businessman and an exceptional mentor, and his guidance and insight proved invaluable throughout my career in London.

Don had warned me early on when I became a CEO in 2007 that I might face such moral crossroads, preparing me for a test that many might not anticipate. Don epitomized what a great mentor should be – an individual whose own character illuminated a path for mentees to navigate most business challenges and important ethical dilemmas. He was fiercely intelligent, understated and elegant, with a down-to-earth disposition and an innate ability to connect with people across all levels of business – you were always laughing when Don was around. He was so professional and took things seriously, but never himself.

Sadly, a decade after we met, Don passed away in 2018. I feel deep gratitude for the friendship we forged and the lessons he imparted. In hindsight, I sometimes wonder whether he had orchestrated the brown bag encounter to test my resolve. Did he, perhaps in collaboration with the partner, seek to test the character of this new CEO? Could he trust this young CEO to always do the right thing to protect the business, employees, shareholders and his direct investment? While it's unlikely that Don was behind this brown bag event, the thought underscores the pivotal role of mentorship in shaping one's character.

## Consistency in character

Reflecting on my journey, it is evident that all my esteemed mentors shared a defining trait: their character remained consistent, both in business and in their personal lives. They rejected the notion that 'it's only business' could excuse callous behaviour when challenges arose. Their character was the same in the office as it was outside the office in daily life.

I also firmly reject the idea that 'it's only business'. As a Stoic striving for personal growth and character perfection, it is impossible to act in contradiction to these principles within a business context.

By displaying a clear pursuit of wisdom, justice, temperance and courage, the CEO can inspire the organization to deliver results for the business but also for themselves to be better along that long career journey. When I consider the lives of Marcus Aurelius and Seneca, this can prove a challenging point. Their public actions were often at odds with their private Stoic beliefs – Marcus' military pursuits against certain German tribes along the Danube have been described at various times as near genocidal. That said, both Marcus and Seneca were products of their times and the requirements of their positions within a brutal system and society. I believe they both demonstrated clear examples of Stoic behaviour and character through their leadership styles and in how they conducted executive actions within legal briefs, which demonstrate extremely balanced hands.

## CEO leadership is a complicated journey

The journey of a CEO is an intricate tapestry woven from all the choices made throughout a career, etched with experiences of success and failure that build character. As we explore the principles of Stoic philosophy, the emphasis on character becomes increasingly apparent. A Stoic CEO recognizes that the path to lasting success is not paved solely through good strategic, tactical and financial business decisions but equally through unwavering integrity, open communication and commitment to embodying the virtues of wisdom, justice, temperance and courage throughout all of those business decisions.

As a business leader, character is not just an abstract ideal – it is a practical necessity. By embracing the Stoic approach to character-building, by making consistent decisions through the lens of the four virtues, CEOs can navigate the complexities of their roles, instilling trust and resilience in their organizations while leading with clarity and purpose. The true measure of a leader lies not merely in their accomplishments but in the strength of their character, which guides them through both triumph and adversity.

## Summary & Reflection

- Integrity is not a style – it is a strategy that supports every consequential decision a CEO will ever make.

- From moral stand-offs in boardrooms to literal bags of cash, my experiences illustrate that leadership without character is an illusion. And character isn't formed in moments of ease but forged in tests of restraint, humility and justice. The mentors who shaped my journey, like Don McCarthy and Richard Gundy, didn't just teach business – they taught me how to develop character.

- The Stoic CEO doesn't hide behind 'just business' excuses. They embody the cardinal virtues – wisdom, justice, courage and temperance – in every quiet decision that never makes headlines but defines legacy.

Chapter 7

# SOCIAL ANIMALS

## JOHN SELLARS

> *What does not benefit the hive is no benefit to the bee.*
>
> Marcus Aurelius, *Meditations* 6.54

## No isolated heroes

There's a certain popular image of the heroic Stoic who has a stiff upper lip, is coldly indifferent to events and resists attachments to other people in order to remain free and invulnerable to the vicissitudes of fortune. When Marcus Aurelius writes that one should 'be like the headland', unharmed by the waves, it is easy to see how such an image could develop.[18] The Stoics certainly had lots to say about how to handle difficult situations – on which more in the coming chapters, especially Chapter 9 – but the image of the Stoic as an isolated heroic figure who goes it alone could not be further from the truth. So, how did the Stoics think about our relationships with other people?

## Social animals

We are animals. Like all other animals, we are ultimately motivated by an instinct for self-preservation. The Stoics built their thinking about human beings on the back of this observation. This might make it sound as if there's an element of selfishness at the heart of Stoicism. However, the Stoics note two things. The first is that our self-preservation inevitably depends on a wide range of people – what newborn baby would survive for very long without the constant help of its parents?

The second is that, if we become parents ourselves, we'll be as concerned for the survival of our children as we are for our own safety. The dependence of children on parents and the love that parents have for their children are both fundamental aspects of human life.

According to one of our most important sources for Stoic ethics, written by the Roman statesman and philosopher Cicero, a parent's love for their children is the foundation of our shared sense of community with other people.[19] This primary and natural instinct highlights our inherent social nature and illustrates the fact that when we are first born we are entirely dependent on others. Cicero goes on say that, from this basic care for offspring, we ought to develop an attitude in which we see all other people as, in some sense, relatives. The human race is ultimately one big family.

## Concentric circles

For the details of how the Stoics explained this idea, we need to turn to another Stoic thinker writing in the Roman period: Hierocles. He too stressed the idea that fundamentally we have an instinct for self-preservation, but we also extend this to our immediate family members and can be as protective of their wellbeing as we are of our own. However, given that our survival depends on the wellbeing of those in our immediate community as well – the people who grow the food we eat, provide clean water and so on – we ought to care about their survival too.

Hierocles suggests that we ought to pull them closer to us, treating them *as if* they were family members.[20] Beyond these close neighbours there are others, further out, who might seem less important to us, but again Hierocles suggest that we try to pull these people closer to us. If these different groups of people fall into a series of concentric circles – close family, extended family, neighbours, fellow citizens – then he says that we should contract these circles, bringing everyone closer to the centre. In the series of circles that Hierocles describes, the largest, outermost circle contains all humankind. The goal is to increase our sense of kinship with everyone else in the world, understanding that we are all members of a single global community.

## Cosmopolitanism

This idea of a single global community goes back to the beginnings of Stoicism. In the decades before its founder, Zeno, arrived in Athens, Alexander the Great had conquered much of the eastern Mediterranean world and the Middle East, spreading Greek culture far and wide. After his death, this vast new territory was divided into three large kingdoms by his successors. The traditional Greek cities no longer had the political autonomy they once did, and people started to see themselves as parts of a much larger, interconnected world. Around the same time, a philosopher called Diogenes proclaimed that he was no longer a citizen of any particular city but instead a citizen of the cosmos – a cosmopolitan.

It was within this radically new political climate that Zeno first came to Athens. Many other leading Stoics also came to Athens from cities within the vast territory conquered by Alexander. These immigrants and converts to Greek culture embraced Diogenes' idea that they did not belong to any particular city, whether that be Athens or the city where they were born, but instead were citizens of the cosmos and members of a single global community. Far from cutting themselves off from other people, the Stoics stressed their connection with all human beings.

## Marcus Aurelius, global citizen

As Emperor of Rome, Marcus Aurelius was unambiguously in charge – the leader of the Western world. Yet, on the few occasions when he directly comments on his role, he seems to downplay it. At one point, he remarks that as Marcus Aurelius he is a Roman, but as a human being he is a citizen of the cosmos.[21] Yes, Marcus was a Roman, the most powerful Roman of all, but more important than that was his place within the community of humankind. He is quite clear about the order of priority: *first*, he is a human being; only second is he a Roman and an emperor. Should the two ever come into conflict, Marcus knows where his top priority lies. Never put the job above being a good, decent human being.

Some readers are often surprised by how little Marcus explicitly says about his role as emperor. Yet that hasn't stopped people in positions of leadership and power taking valuable lessons from it; as we noted earlier, US President Bill Clinton once said that the *Meditations* influenced him more than any other book.[22] The lessons that we can take from Marcus come not from comments about his own experience of political leadership but from his wider reflections on our place within the wider community of all people. In multiple places, Marcus compares the community of all humankind to a living organism made up of parts. Each person is a part of this community and has a role to play. In fact, in a play on words, Marcus goes further: it is not good enough merely to be a part (*meros*); we must see ourselves as limbs (*melos*) of this organic unity.[23] Just as a foot has no purpose or function when cut off from the body, a human being cut off and isolated from others can no longer be a human being in the fullest sense. Again and again, Marcus reminds himself that he is not a unique singular leader but instead simply one part – one limb – within the wider community.

In these reflections, Marcus is thinking about humankind as a whole, but the same thought applies at multiple different levels. Whatever the size or type of community, organization or team, each member – including the leader – is just one component in the larger whole. And building on this thought, Marcus insists that it is the wellbeing of that larger entity that matters most and ought to be the focus of every member in it. If we are fully integrated 'limbs', then our success and wellbeing will be dependent on the wellbeing of the 'organism' as a whole. The foot severed from the body cannot survive on its own; its very existence as a foot depends on it being part of the human body. Similarly, a leader can only be a leader if they are within a team or organization. The success of the leader and the group are intimately connected.

Chapter 8

# STOIC TEAMWORK IN BUSINESS

## JUSTIN STEAD

> *Associate with people who are likely to improve you.*
>
> Seneca, *Letters* 7.8

I often laugh at how business titans present themselves to the public. There are certain figures who are only associated with the company they founded. Rarely do you hear this omnipresent figure utter more than a few clichéd 'incredible team' comments about their workforce, key executives or the people who actually deliver the success of the company. There are thousands of people in these businesses doing an incredible job, and certainly the senior management team must be very accomplished as individual business leaders. It is as if no one else works there! There is minimal praise but certainly plenty of critique within what are often very demanding cultures. The results have been incredible – let's not lose sight of this fact. Good for the businesses themselves, but it's hard to say how good they are for the human beings in those businesses and society as a whole.

Every leader needs to have a great team around them. Augustus, widely regarded as the greatest emperor of them all, had Marcus Agrippa – his 'chief operating officer' – to deliver his vision. It was Agrippa who won the decisive battle at Actium to consolidate Augustus' power over Mark Antony and Cleopatra, and ultimately the entire Roman Empire. Agrippa also led massive public works projects in Rome, transforming it from a city of bricks to a city of marble – Augustus' dream. Augustus, although not a Stoic himself, valued Stoic philosophy greatly. This is evidenced by his reliance on two key Stoic advisers: Athenodorus Cananites and Arius Didymus, who helped him cultivate patience and shape his character to rule Rome wisely.

The Stoic model of leadership through teamwork is quite different from that of current role models we see both in business and in political arenas. At its core, the message is 'Less me and more we', using the cardinal virtues to bring like-minded people together to harmonize and accomplish great things. The cornerstones of a Stoic team are:

1. Low ego with the understanding that it's not about me.

2. Tactical clarity in decision-making, guided by the company strategy and the four cardinal virtues.

3. All voices are welcome, even dissenting ones, as long as the team agrees on the overall strategy and shared core personal values.

4. Collaboration and listening are essential to form bonds within the team.

5. Harmony is victory – we don't sweat the small stuff, and sometimes not even the big stuff, if it means preserving unity.

## Marcus Aurelius as a team leader

Marcus Aurelius was a true team player. From the *Meditations*, his legal briefs and his letters to Fronto – his great mentor – we see that he was calm, polite, engaging, detailed, deliberate and considered, yet a person of significant energy and action.

In particular, he knew as a Stoic that he was the custodian of power, not the instrument of power, and that moderation not domination was his standard. For this approach, he was admired and respected by his team, the Senate and the people of Rome.

All these qualities instilled a great sense of loyalty in his team, who had to execute his strategy at a time when trust was absolutely essential because communication across the Empire could take weeks or months.

Marcus endorsed a system of trust, but he was also extremely pragmatic and hands-on when required, like a CEO in a crisis. The following examples demonstrate Marcus' leadership style:

- **Sharing power from day one:** On day one of his emperorship, Marcus expanded the executive team immediately by making his brother, Verus, co-emperor. He went as far as telling the Senate that if Verus wasn't elevated, he would not proceed as emperor. This was a bold move, and his Senate 'advisory board' team backed him.

- **Strategic pragmatism:** Once Verus was confirmed, Marcus offered the Praetorian Guard one of the largest donatives ever. Was this a bribe? Was he buying loyalty? Perhaps. But it was a pragmatic move to consolidate power, stabilize the Empire and ensure a smooth transition to a new 'senior executive team'.

- ▶ **Being present where needed:** Marcus supported his team by being present where he was needed most. He stayed in Rome while Verus went east to deal with the Parthians. Later, despite no prior military experience, Marcus stood on the front line with his troops along the Danube, ensuring they had his full support to fight the Germanic tribes. In a short period of time, he became a highly effective military general.

- ▶ **Maintaining loyalty in crisis:** When Avidius Cassius declared himself emperor in Syria, mistakenly thinking Marcus was dead, Marcus marched east hoping to forgive his friend and avoid civil war. Remarkably, most other generals stayed loyal to Marcus – a testament to the clarity of his vision, the inclusion of his leadership team and the strong bonds he had cultivated.

- ▶ **Encouraging debate and listening:** Marcus encouraged debate and discussion in his team. He was known as a patient listener, as is evident in the legal briefs we can still read today. Everyone wants to know that the CEO is listening – it builds powerful bonds. His discernment and courage to listen to his team and do what was best for the Empire, even when in conflict with Stoic ideals, showed significant leadership qualities.

During my CEO roles, I often thought carefully about these traits of Marcus. As I formed, developed and worked with teams all over the world throughout my career, these Stoic leadership concepts guided me, leading to fantastic results at Fossil Watch Group and Watches of Switzerland – more on that in Chapter 14.

## Marcus' lessons in team building for a CEO

### 1. Sharing power and the executive limelight

Marcus shared executive power and the stage with Verus. When I became CEO, I made sure that at any company or partner event, the team spoke in equal measure alongside me. Everyone on the senior leadership team needed – and, for the most part, wanted – to speak. This made us look and act like a well-coordinated team, aligned with the company objectives, not just the CEO's desires. It also brought out leadership qualities in the team, building confidence as they shared the stage and owned the message together.

### 2. Making pragmatic decisions to strengthen the team

Marcus had to 'buy off' the Praetorian Guard to secure his tenure. Some might see this as un-Stoic, but I see it as pragmatic and sensible. Likewise, I have had to 'buy in' expertise or pay above market rates to secure vital talent. In one case, I approved an executive earning more than me, the CEO, because I believed their value to the business and shareholders was mission-critical. It proved to be a wise decision.

## 3. Knowing when and where the team needs you most

Marcus moved across the Empire, personally overseeing crucial operations and tending to day-to-day matters in Rome. I don't need to be in every place at every moment as a CEO. I need to be where I am most needed, in a way that aligns with what my team expects. With a clear strategy and great people, the day-to-day within each area largely manages itself. I always divide my one-on-ones into three buckets:

- ▶ What do you want to tell me confidently, knowing you are fully in control? (wisdom)

- ▶ What would you like to discuss, knowing you already have a solution but would like my opinion? (justice and temperance)

- ▶ What worries you or where do you feel uncertain and need my help or decision? (courage)

This Stoic approach builds clarity and trust, while allowing me to support each team member in a way that works for them.

## 4. Building loyalty and accepting losses

Marcus reminds us in *Meditations* 2.1 that we must work with people of all persuasions and motivations.

> *Begin the morning by saying to thyself, I shall meet with the busybody, the ungrateful, arrogant, deceitful, envious, unsocial ... I can neither be injured by any of them, nor can I be angry with my kinsman, nor hate him. For we are made for cooperation ... To act against one another then is contrary to nature; and it is acting against one another to be vexed and to turn away.*
>
> Marcus Aurelius, *Meditations* 2.1

A great team isn't a room full of clones – quite the opposite. I believe 'culture eats strategy for breakfast'. Culture starts at the top, with clear values set by the CEO and reinforced by the senior leadership team. I never wanted people just like me. I focused on bringing in technical experts to cover my weaknesses and prioritized values when hiring. Sometimes, I chose less technically perfect candidates who were simply better humans – people who would help build a values-driven culture.

## 5. Communication: Stoic civility builds team harmony

'It's not what you say but how you say it.' Disagreements and conflicts are inevitable, but how they are resolved defines team health. Hard issues require direct, honest and civil communication. The option to 'agree to disagree' should always be available, without a complete fallout.

## 6. Debate is crucial

When I took over my first major enterprise as CEO, my CFO, Steve Sargent, nearly drove me crazy. Steve was a smart physics major from Essex who, in my eyes, seemed to drain momentum from the room, with what I perceived as negativity, whenever I proposed new initiatives in a business that needed a significant cultural reset. At first, I thought he was a blocker. But over time, I realized he wasn't trying to sabotage progress – he was a much-needed cautionary brake. Steve embodied the Stoic idea of *praemeditatio futurorum malorum* – anticipating what could go wrong and preparing for it.

We had many tough conversations, but Steve stayed patient with me, and I learned to value his perspective deeply. Over time, we became strong partners. Eventually, I did almost nothing without his sober second look. A great CFO with a cautionary mindset is an immense asset to a hard-charging CEO and a wonderful balance in the broader commercial team.

## The true strength of a Stoic-led team

Building a great Stoic-led team takes careful consideration, humility, courage and patience. You must share the stage, include all voices (even when they sting) and support each other when things get tough, all through a shared commitment to strategy and values. It is the upfront setup and commitment to the strategy, as well as the shared behavioural values, that hold the team and business together when things are tough.

When a crisis hits, or when the lights are bright, it is the quiet strength of the team standing behind you that truly defines success. As Marcus Aurelius knew, no leader – no matter how talented or visionary – wins alone.

## Summary & Reflection

▶ The Stoic leader is not a lone visionary but the heartbeat of a harmonious, values-driven team. Through the example of Marcus Aurelius, we see that the highest expression of leadership is not dominance but collaboration.

▶ By sharing the spotlight and fostering open communication, the Stoic CEO can build a culture where every voice matters and every decision is filtered through the virtues of wisdom, justice, courage and temperance.

▶ Great businesses are built by disciplined, aligned teams that move with unity, even amid complexity and conflict. The Stoic leader knows when to act, when to listen and when to stand back and let others step forward.

▶ The boardroom is not a battlefield – it's a forum, and its greatest strength lies in its collective virtue.

Chapter 9

# FACING CHALLENGES

## JOHN SELLARS

> *Whatever may come about, it is within my power to derive benefit from it.*
>
> Epictetus, *Handbook* 18
>
> \*
>
> *Disaster is virtue's opportunity!*
>
> Seneca, *On Providence* 4.6

## Shipwrecks

Stoic philosophy began with a shipwreck. As we saw earlier, the first Stoic philosopher Zeno had been travelling to Athens with cargo from his father's business when his ship sank. Fortunately, Zeno survived and was able to get to shore. Although he had lost all his merchandise, he still had with him the things that matter most: his knowledge and his character. With these, he could easily build a new life. This brings to mind a famous saying by the Greek philosopher Aristippus: 'Parents should provide for their children wealth and travelling equipment of such a kind, that, even after shipwreck, it can swim to land along with them.'[24] Aristippus was no Stoic but at least agreed with them on this point. Given this dramatic experience, perhaps it should not be so surprising that Zeno went on to develop a philosophy that stressed the importance of character over material possessions.

Zeno was not the only Stoic to face difficult events. Indeed, he wasn't even the only Stoic to suffer shipwreck – Seneca was probably on board a fateful trip across the Mediterranean in which his uncle died.[25] Seneca was, from one perspective, extremely privileged; he was well educated, moved in the highest social circles, was one of the richest people in Rome in his day, and he had considerable political influence at the highest level. Yet at the same time, he had to deal with the death of his father, the threat of execution, long-term illness, the death of his son, an extended period of exile, the death of a close friend, an impossible job as tutor and then adviser to Nero (a role from which he couldn't easily resign), and ultimately he was forced to commit suicide. If anyone knew about adversity, it was Seneca.

Marcus Aurelius faced many challenges too. During his lifetime, plague ravaged the Roman Empire, he dealt with the adversities of war and, on a more personal level, he and his wife, Faustina, had a total of fourteen children, of which only four are known to have made it to adulthood. When Marcus comments that when someone loses a child they should think of this as simply giving them back to where they came from – Nature – he was not being an unfeeling, insensitive philosopher; instead, he was consoling himself as he confronted one of the most painful situations anyone can face.

In response to the challenges he faced, Marcus encouraged himself to stand firm and not be shaken by such events.

> *Be like the headland, on which the waves break constantly, which still stands firm, while the foaming waters are put to rest around it. 'It is my bad luck that this has happened to me.' On the contrary, say, 'It is my good luck that, although this has happened to me, I can bear it without getting upset, neither crushed by the present nor afraid of the future.' This kind of event could have happened to anyone, but not everyone would have borne it without getting upset.*
>
> Marcus Aurelius, *Meditations* 4.49

This is an example of resilience – not being disturbed by external events. But it was not the only Stoic response to adversity.

## Learning from adversity

Seneca faced the sorts of challenges in his life that hopefully few of us will ever have to experience. How did he react to them? His first response was to insist that none of these things truly harmed him. They might undermine his reputation, hamper his career or take away his possessions, but none of them could damage what matters most: his character.[26] Like Marcus, Seneca encouraged himself to be unmoved by external events. However, he did not want to leave it at that. Seneca wanted to find a way to turn what seemed like an unambiguous negative into a positive.

He did this by suggesting that we ought to see difficult events not merely as turbulence to be endured, but instead as training that improves and strengthens us. The only way to develop skills in any area of life is to have them tested. Seneca gives the example of a wrestler who can only develop his skills through constant training, which will inevitably be tough and often involve losing. But it is only by going through this process that the wrestler will develop the skills he needs in order to start winning. There is no shortcut.

The wrestler in training will welcome the hard work and regular defeats he faces, knowing that this is the only way to improve. Once he has developed those skills, he will continue to welcome tough opponents so he can show off his ability and keep himself at the top of his game. Indeed, if he were only ever to face other wrestlers who were significantly below his standard, he would soon get bored and complacent. For this reason, a good wrestler will seek out the best opponents he can find.

> *Those things which you call hardships, which you call adversities and accursed, are, in the first place, for the good of the persons themselves to whom they come.*
>
> Seneca, *On Providence* 3.1

In this way, Seneca argues that not only can we *benefit* from difficult challenges, but they are in fact *necessary* if we are to learn. Once we see that, he suggests that we ought to *welcome* them, knowing that they are essential, character-forming experiences.

> *No one seems to me more unhappy than one who has never met with adversity.*
>
> Demetrius, quoted by Seneca[27]

This can seem like overstatement. There are some things that no one would ever want to welcome, such as the loss of a loved one. But Seneca pulls no punches: the only way to learn how to handle grief, he comments, is to go through it.

It is clear that Seneca thinks these ideas can be translated into any area of life. In the context of leadership, one can easily imagine what he would say:

- ▶ Adversity is inevitable, so all leaders should expect to face challenges.

- ▶ A good leader will want to face challenges, because this is the only way to develop and grow as a leader.

- ▶ The only way to know if you are a good leader is to have one's skills put to the test in difficult situations.

The most unfortunate person, Seneca says, is the one who has never been tested. To them he says, 'No one will know what you can do, not even yourself.'[28]

## Beyond resilience

In his book *Antifragile*, Nassim Taleb notes that people often assume that the opposite of fragility is resilience.[29] The defining characteristic of something fragile is that it is prone to break, whereas something resilient is unaffected and can withstand most bumps and knocks. Taleb argues that it is a mistake to think of these as opposites: the true opposite of something prone to break when put under stress would be something that benefitted or got stronger from stress. No word exists for such a thing, so Taleb calls it 'antifragile'. In light of this, we can say that there are three types of thing: the fragile (prone to break in adverse situations); the resilient (indifferent to circumstances); and the antifragile (benefits from adverse situations).

Seneca's view is a clear example of what Taleb describes as antifragility. Taleb applies this to a wide variety of domains – businesses, cities, countries, biological organisms – reflecting on whether it is possible for something not merely to become resilient to adversity but to positively benefit from it.

Of course, most of us would much prefer to avoid those sorts of difficult situations altogether, even if we acknowledged that in some ways we might benefit from them. But the blunt fact is that adversity is coming, whether we like it or not. Life does not always go the way we would like it to: sometimes our plans will fail, we'll get sick, larger events out of our control might upset the certainties of daily life, loved ones will die. These are not disasters but simply the inevitable ups and downs that shape everyone's lives. We'll face adversity at some point. So if we can actually find a way to benefit from it, or at least to see that some benefit can be taken from difficult situations, then we'll hopefully be able to navigate them better. We may never reach the point that Seneca describes of actively welcoming adversity – perhaps he was overstating this for rhetorical effect – but it may lessen the blow. It may also help us to see in hindsight that in fact we have learned something valuable and grown in the wake of the challenges we have faced.

―― FACING CHALLENGES ――

# Preparing for challenges

Adversity comes in many forms. Perhaps the worst, and the one people fear most, is death. In *Meditations*, Marcus Aurelius often reflects on his own impending death. As he got older, Marcus struggled with his health; given the limited medical knowledge of the time, it was difficult to know what was and was not a life-threatening condition. Writing in his fifties, suffering from various ailments, he was all too conscious that at some point his life would come to an end. In these reflections, he reminds himself of the following:

- As a mortal human being he must, like everyone else, die at some point. That's just a consequence of being alive.

- Death is a completely natural event, like the cycle from day to night or the passing of the seasons. It's nothing bad in itself.

- Nature is constantly changing; nothing stays the same forever.

- He cannot change the fact that one day he must die, but he can enjoy his life and live it to the fullest right now in the present moment.

Death and bereavement are extreme cases of adversity, although they are ones that we all must face at some point. But we face countless other examples of adversity that upset us, leave us stressed and annoyed, and sometimes make us angry with other people.

The Stoics had a technique designed to help us cope with such situations. It is known as preparation for future evils (*praemeditatio futurorum malorum*). Think about some event that you are likely to encounter today, perhaps an event you often have to deal with and that sometimes upsets you when it goes wrong. Now imagine the worst-case scenario: the train is cancelled and you can't get to work; the internet connection goes down just before an important online meeting; the delivery you were depending on doesn't show up. How would you feel? How bad would it really be? What would you do in response if this actually happened? Remind yourself of some of the Stoic ideas we have encountered already, in particular the thought that we are not disturbed by things but by the judgements we make about them.

Stoics such as Marcus Aurelius used to do this each morning, mentally preparing for things that might go wrong in the coming day. There are a number of potential benefits from doing this:

▶ If things do go wrong and you have already mentally rehearsed that scenario, then it won't hit you so hard emotionally. You knew in advance that this was a possible outcome.

▶ Part of your rehearsal can include planning for what you'd do in such a situation. With that back-up plan already in place, you can swiftly and calmly shift to plan B.

▶ If things go well, you'll be all the more grateful and happy because you haven't taken this outcome for granted.

Chapter 10

# THE JOURNEY TO BECOME A STOIC LEADER

## JUSTIN STEAD

> *It is a rough road that leads to the heights of greatness.*
>
> Seneca, *On Providence* 4.10

Pat Cash was a professional tennis player celebrated for his exploits on the court, which culminated in his 1987 Wimbledon Championship win. But for me, as an aspiring tennis professional at the lower ends of the tour and club leagues in Germany in the mid-'80s, he was much more. He was an Australian icon who represented the best attributes of our country – he was tough, resilient, ambitious, courageous, competitive, loyal to a fault, values-driven and so generous to friends and family.

Pat had to overcome some brutal injuries during his career, alongside many difficult challenges off the court. What he had to go through to become a champion tennis player and human being is the definition of Stoic resilience and dedication. For me, if you looked up 'Stoicism' in the Oxford English Dictionary, you could simply place an image of Epictetus, who carried injuries from his broken leg, and Pat Cash and say nothing else.

As I got to know Pat very well as a best mate over the past twenty years, I have come to admire him even more for the person he is now than for his tennis accomplishments. He is a co-founder of the Aurelius Foundation, a charity created to raise awareness of Stoic principles, and we do many presentations and events on Stoicism together. His testimonies and life stories leave audiences in complete awe – alongside another Wimbledon champion, Boris Becker, who is also a convert to Stoicism through the Aurelius Foundation. Between them they have an incredible set of life stories that capture Stoic resilience and overcoming life's challenges in remarkable, profound and pragmatic ways. In Chapter 19, we will come back to Pat, Boris and a remarkable Stoic meeting at HMP Huntercombe in December 2022.

Recently, Pat and I were discussing Stoic challenge management with a group of more than fifty CEOs in London. I was asked why I did not make it as a tennis player but did make it as a successful CEO. And conversely, why did Pat make it as one of the best players in the world in his era? This is very easy to answer from an athletic standpoint. As Sam Mussabini aptly put it in the movie *Chariots of Fire*, when talking to the great Harold Abrahams about improving his speed over the 100m dash: 'Mr Abrahams, you cannot put in what God left out!'

In my case, the Good Lord gave me athletic skills for which I am forever grateful – sport is among the great joys of my life. But there is a huge difference between an athlete like me and a truly elite athlete like Pat Cash. Athletes like Pat are like a modern-day Achilles – the ultimate Greek warrior.

So, this is a true and obvious reason I did not advance past an ATP world ranking of 400. But there was another significant reason: I simply did not have the emotional control to compete day-to-day on the professional tennis tour in my early twenties. At that stage of my life, I lacked the emotional awareness and advanced Stoic toolkit to stabilize myself match after match without each one feeling like a huge emotional burden.

When I started to calm down and strike a Stoic balance towards the end of my tennis career, I played some of my best matches ever. Pat and Boris played at their level in some other universe, partly due to their immense physical gifts, but also thanks to their mental and emotional skill sets and resilience on court.

They had to develop their emotional resilience on court with a process over years – mine would come later in a different arena.

## The gift of tennis for business

My years playing tennis proved massively helpful when I entered the workforce at the age of twenty-six as an executive trainee at Payless Shoes in Topeka, Kansas. My first week on the job was spent working in the storeroom of a Payless store in Kansas City, unpacking ladies' $9 Chinese work 'pumps' and placing them on racks. Fourteen years later, I was the CEO of one of the most important luxury retailers in the world in London, in the global watch and jewellery industry.

The first twelve months as CEO of this business in London were brutal in every way – the business was 'on fire' everywhere. Overstocked inventory, low cash, banking covenants about to break, creditors circling, suppliers working against the business and against me personally, brand partners leaving the business, others threatening to, and one of the worst cultures you could encounter. Yet, the way I saw the situation was different from most people. My mindset was, 'Good. This needs to be fixed! This is exactly what I am here to work through, and it can be only up from here.' Critically, it was not fourteen years of professional experience that gave me the confidence to 'dive into the arena and compete', as important as they had been. It was the arduous and emotional tennis journey that prepared me for this daunting set of business challenges.

The challenges I encountered during my tennis career had helped me build a well-developed Stoic toolkit. So when I entered this major professional fray, I was able to remain reasonably steady throughout, control my emotions, stabilize problems, convert partnerships positively and work people to my corner to eventually overcome these difficult hurdles. I had an inner citadel, a place of serenity within – even if it was not always evident to those around me. This citadel was forged on tennis courts all around the world, mostly thanks to failing.

Armed with my Stoic toolkit, my exceptional team and I turned the business around. I was fortunate to inherit a set of people who possessed terrific expertise and abilities and just needed to be led correctly. After exiting troublemakers, this team was an outstanding example of 'the sum of the parts' being complementary and outstanding together. I owe them so much for the success we enjoyed that culminated in me lifting my own personal 'Wimbledon Trophy' by selling to Apollo Private Equity in 2012. This outcome confirmed a wonderful financial return for the shareholders, secured the company's long-term financial future and delivered life-changing events for many on the team.

## Reality management and the abyss of social media

Life is tough, complicated and does not give anyone too many free lunches. Even those who are perceived to have it all can struggle to manage it well – the list of business leaders, sports stars and celebrities seeing their lives collapse due to poor personal decisions is endless. Why? Because regardless of circumstance, race, ethnicity or socioeconomic status, we are all human beings with beating hearts, desiring minds and yearning souls. Life is a daily challenge to manage ourselves correctly as we interact with our individual worlds and exist alongside 8 billion other people, all facing the same challenges.

The advent of social media has amplified and distorted reality and placed different pressures on people – especially young people. The overwhelming reality distortion comes from a disproportionate amount of 'fakery' that exists in what people are willing to share about the 'truth' of their reality. There is a major pursuit of pleasure over happiness and a misconception of how hard it is to be excellent in a chosen calling. The focus on building a career based on 'influencing' and 'likes' has created a vicious circle of negativity, with social media platforms creating addictive algorithms that feed an endless stream of fakery, resulting in commercial returns for both the facilitators and content providers, often at the expense of consumers.

The social media environment itself is challenging enough, let alone the knock-on effects on how people interact and communicate today. Many believe they can say what they want, when they want, to anyone they want, without reasonable concern for discourse and civility. The 'keyboard warrior' mentality and 'comparison culture' have both run amok. Social media is contributing to well-documented mental health issues across society, especially in young people who do not have fully developed critical thinking skills to discern 'brain rot' from truth or facts.

Seneca warned us 2,000 years ago about the danger of easy access and luxury and what it does to a person.

> *Our luxuries have condemned us to weakness; we have ceased to be able to do that which we have long declined to do.*
>
> Seneca, *Letters* 55.1

Social media perpetuates these falsehoods, with charlatans promising the easy life if you 'follow me'. Social media is a haven for this world of mistrust.

## Where do we turn?

So, where can we turn for solutions or the right process to overcome life's challenges? How should we approach all our challenges as human beings, regardless of our status or position in society – champion athletes, famous celebrities, powerful CEOs or the richest people in the world?

The Stoics are clear, and Seneca in particular is very clear: we can turn to Nature itself to provide us with answers, considering Her most basic rules, Her physics and Her inner workings.

## Stoic mindset: A challenge is a learning opportunity

We shield our children from hardship because we do not want to see them hurt or damaged. In the business world, mental health issues are at a crisis point, and managers must be so careful in guarding the interests of their teams. Within both of these spheres, there is a duty of care, but where is the balance to allow children and people to feel the right amount of pressure and challenge to enable them to grow, learn and mature?

The irony is that so many young people want to do great things, be famous and accomplish something with their lives – these are wonderful goals if the intention is elite development of craft rather than material outcomes. The journey of understanding and the equation for being successful have been lost, often through and because of social media. Struggle, failure, loss, pain and pressure can be used as learning experiences, from which you can take courage to improve and refine your abilities. You are in a process and cycle of improvement, and it is important to recognize this process and stick with it.

Despite societal misunderstandings, the business world keeps a close eye on reality – known as the bottom line. When money is at stake and the motivation behind the deployment of capital and financial investment is scrutinized, a key point of confidence is that the CEO and leadership are capable, motivated and *proven*.

And 'proven' is an experiential characteristic that cannot be cheated or manufactured via a shortcut. Certainly, there are other important characteristics for a CEO, but looking through the experience of a manager is a strong indicator of their capacity to cope with and absorb the endless stresses of the CEO role.

## Marcus Aurelius and patience

Marcus Aurelius was incredibly patient before taking over the emperorship of Rome. He had a long time to prove himself, as he was too young to assume the throne after Hadrian died. The agreement was for Antoninus Pius to be placed on the throne in the interim, specifically to prepare Marcus for the role as his adopted son. The issue was that it became a 23-year wait until Antoninus finally died! That must have been a challenge for Marcus' patience, but he used the time to learn and prove he was a justified choice to be emperor.

When Marcus finally assumed the throne, he stepped into a most difficult set of circumstances as chair and CEO of the Roman Empire – war, plague, economic downturn, betrayal by his best general. At one point, Marcus was even selling off parts of the imperial household furniture to raise state funds. Marcus was forty years old when he became emperor, and although not tested operationally at that level, he had been prepared extremely well to rule. He had been through a robust educational and practical process, learning how to govern and rule while being very well-mentored – he proved he could be patient, and it served him well.

## Amor fati: Accept and love your fate

Proven leaders learn through their journey to embrace the concept of *amor fati*.[30] *Amor fati*, a deep-rooted Stoic theme meaning 'love of fate', is the concept of accepting and embracing everything that happens in one's life – including suffering and loss – as good, or at least necessary. It involves not just enduring but actively loving one's fate, viewing all life events as meaningful and purposeful. This encourages a mindset of acceptance and resilience in the face of adversity.

> *Do not seek to have everything happen as you wish, but wish for everything to happen as it does, and your life will flow well.*
>
> Epictetus, *Handbook* 8

I had to make some significant changes to my outlook and personal philosophy over the years to fully adopt this concept – I was always too optimistic in my early career with my financial forecasts and how I presented them to management. I made a lot of mistakes, and it hurt me and the business. Being an Australian and an American-trained professional, I was only half the coin – too positive and not enough 'what if?' in my make-up, always wanting smoother sailing. I had to adopt *amor fati* as a core management principle to improve my leadership skills, and it has become the foundation for my chair leadership roles.

The best CEOs adopt this principle as a core professional and self-management tool. They have been forged in the cauldron and pressurized in the school of hard knocks, so they are prepared to deal with responsibilities and circumstances that come from expected and unexpected places.

The buck stops with the CEO. Every issue should be approached with calm and collected reasoning: good news, bad news – it's all just news. The key is what happens next. Within the context of a focused and disciplined strategy, decisions are made accordingly to reduce risk and maximize opportunities.

At present, I work with five founders and CEOs as an investor and chair, and one very large private company as the chair. The CEOs I work with today are great business professionals but even better people – I choose who I work with and invest in very carefully nowadays. There are no guarantees in business, just best forecasts, but the character of a CEO is an excellent compass when looking at new businesses.

Business is a tough and highly competitive arena, and if you are working with a difficult human being, be prepared for a long day – I find myself constantly referring to Marcus' *Meditations* 2.1 (see page 99). My teams work within a disciplined macro system of management to capitalize on their opportunity over time, but I always encourage them to embrace everything happening across their entire business (good and bad) and to stop looking for perfection and calm seas – this a reality that will never materialize.

The next major macroeconomic disruption triggered by a global unforeseen event – like the 2007 Global Financial Crisis, 2016 Brexit vote or the 2020 Covid pandemic – is no doubt around the corner. But our system of management, our mindset to adapt and improve, our openness to change and our collective Stoic calmness will see us through to our best possible outcomes and results. And when we have periods of success, we look to maximize and consolidate these periods just as we do when we are fighting for survival.

I keep reminding my partners – and therefore myself – that it is the journey, not the destination, that makes the character of a great person. This is a Stoic's greatest reward. As Seneca reminds me constantly: 'Not one of the things we have is necessary; only let us return to the law of nature and riches are ready and waiting.'

## Summary & Reflection

- ▶ Greatness is forged in hardship, not in spite of it. Whether in the arena of elite sport or the furnace of a crisis, the Stoic leader doesn't avoid suffering, they learn from it.

- ▶ From my fledgling tennis career in Germany to my time as a CEO in the boardrooms of London, I used my failures to learn Stoic emotional control. What separates world-class performers from the rest is not just skill – but the capacity to remain resilient and to respond with calm conviction, rather than an impulsive reaction.

- The concept of *amor fati* is not passive acceptance; it's the act of embracing life's challenges and the quest to find meaning and purpose in them. This is a CEO's daily task: not to bend the world to our expectations but to respond to challenges with clarity, patience and strength.

Chapter 11

# STOIC DECISION-MAKING

## JOHN SELLARS

> *Whatever you do, do it with goodness, in the sense of what it means to be a good person. Hold on to this in everything you do.*
>
> Marcus Aurelius, *Meditations* 4.10

We have already seen in Chapter 5 that the Stoics thought the greatest benefit a person can have is a virtuous character. Having the right frame of mind is *always* a good thing, whether circumstances are good or bad. What we can call 'external benefits' – money, success, health, good reputation – are not essential for a good life, the Stoics argued. However, that does not mean that they were completely indifferent to them, despite calling them 'indifferents'. Positive things like health and money they called 'preferred', while negative things such as illness and poverty were 'dispreferred'. A virtuous character might be the most important factor, but as we all know, much of daily life is taken up with thinking about external matters – pursuing what we need and avoiding what might harm us. Indeed, the whole point of cultivating a virtuous character is to give you the skills to make sensible choices when pursuing and avoiding the external.

> 'Are we to use these external things in a careless fashion?' Not at all, for that is bad for our faculty of choice and thus against nature. Instead, they should be used carefully, because their use is not a matter of indifference ... [even though] the material being used is indifferent.
>
> Epictetus, *Discourses* 2.5.6–7

The image of the Stoic as someone totally focused on their inner virtue and indifferent to the world around them misses this key point. The only reason to care about virtue in the first place is so that we can become more effective in how we make use of things in the external world, guided by careful reasoning and a firm set of moral principles.

## Stoic case studies

Cicero's *On Duties* is a practical guide to how to live like a Stoic. Cicero wrote it as a guidebook for his son and based it closely on a now lost work by the Stoic Panaetius. Among the many practical questions that it discusses, one of the most striking is how to resolve apparent conflicts between what is the right thing to do and what will bring us benefits.

As we've already seen, strictly speaking there is no conflict here: doing the right thing – acting virtuously – always brings the greatest benefit. But Cicero is more concerned with the everyday dilemmas that people face when trying to decide what to do. Where should we draw the line between pursuing external benefits and acting virtuously?

### CASE STUDY 1: THE GRAIN SHIP
Consider the following example, which Cicero tells us was discussed by two leading Stoics – Diogenes of Babylon and Antipater of Tarsus.[31] A grain merchant was importing a large

amount of corn from Alexandria to the island of Rhodes. There had been a shortage of corn in Rhodes and as a consequence the price was high. The merchant had the potential to make a good sale. However, if he knew that there were other boats behind his, also loaded with corn and on their way to Rhodes, should he tell his prospective customers, knowing that it will lower the price, or should he benefit from the higher price before they arrive? The merchant is a good, decent man and wants to do the right thing, not make a profit at any cost. But what is the right thing to do?

The Stoic Diogenes of Babylon argued that the merchant was under no obligation to tell his prospective buyers that more ships were on their way. He should be open and honest about his product, and not intentionally deceive, but he was under no obligation to give any further information. The merchant is in business to make money and will of course try to sell his corn at the highest price he can.

Diogenes' pupil, Antipater, disagreed, arguing that the merchant ought to disclose all relevant information, so that his buyers know everything that he does. Although he may be in business to make money, the merchant's first priority ought to be to the interests of his fellow humans and the sense of community he shares with them. Ripping people off is hardly conducive to getting on well with them.

In response to this, Diogenes argued that if Antipater's view was taken to its logical conclusion, we would be morally obliged to give away all our possessions to those in more need than us. While that might be a noble thing to do, it would undermine the very idea of selling corn – or indeed, selling anything – in the first place. We live in a world in which private property exists and people buy and sell things for a profit. The question is what's the right thing to do in the world in which we actually live.

Cicero doesn't tell us who won the debate between Diogenes and Antipater, although he does take Antipater's side – 'What sort of person would hide such highly relevant information?' he asks. We can see two leading Stoics making arguments for both sides of the debate, and so there isn't a clear-cut Stoic answer. The important point is that they are concerned with what is the right thing to do.

Diogenes is *not* suggesting that the merchant stays quiet in order to make a quick profit *at the expense* of doing the right thing. But if it is widely accepted that prices fluctuate and it is entirely appropriate to get the best price the market offers at that moment, then according to Diogenes, there's nothing wrong in doing just that, and the merchant has in no way compromised his character.

## CASE STUDY 2: SELLING YOUR HOUSE

Consider another example, also from Cicero.[32] A man is selling his house. He knows there are problems with it, perhaps damp or a leaking roof. Again, assuming he is a good, decent person, should he disclose these problems to any prospective buyer? Or will he be under no obligation to do so, given that everyone knows it is the buyer's responsibility to inspect the property, have it surveyed and make sure they are happy with it?

Once again, Antipater argued that the buyer ought to disclose everything he knows. Diogenes took the opposite view: no one is forcing the buyer to buy. It is up to them to choose whether or not to buy, and for them to gather information so that they can make an informed decision. The man selling wants to sell his house, so it would be odd to act in a way that undermines achieving that goal. For Diogenes, silence is not deception. However, if someone asked the seller directly, it would of course be unacceptable to lie.

What's the appropriate thing to do? Once again, we have two leading Stoics arguing for opposing views. These cases were highlighted precisely because they are not clear-cut. It is also worth stressing that the debate is not about whether to prioritize personal benefit over acting virtuously. The issue is what counts as virtuous behaviour in complex everyday situations.

## Principles not rules

The lack of a clear answer to these dilemmas highlights a key feature of Stoic ethics: there are no simple rules. There is no Stoic rule book that can tell you what to do in any given situation. This is because every situation is unique and must be assessed on its own terms. For the most part, deception is wrong, but there might be situations in which it becomes the appropriate thing to do if, for instance, it will stop someone from hurting themselves or someone else. A blunt rule like 'never lie' is too simplistic for the wide array of complex situations we encounter in real life.

So, how *do* we decide what to do? Even though there are no rules, there are still guiding principles that we can use to help us make decisions in the real world. There's also a method that we can use to help us avoid mistakes.[33]

## Stage 1: Pause

The first piece of advice the Stoics give is that we ought to pause before deciding to do anything. Many mistakes are the product of hasty and often emotional decisions. The goal is to become calm, considered and thoughtful – to be good, rational beings. If we rush into decisions, we don't give ourselves any time to think about what we ought to be doing.

This connects closely with what the Stoics have to say about emotions. Throughout the day, we are bombarded with experiences that we react to intuitively and instinctively, without thinking – 'this is good', 'this is bad', 'this feels threatening', 'I really want that'. We are continually making immediate and unthinking value judgements about almost everything we experience. If we confirm those judgements in our mind, then they will generate emotions, making us desirous, frightened, angry and more. Then we act on those emotions. All this takes place so fast that we don't even notice it happening.

The problem is that many of those immediate value judgements are wrong. Our instinctive 'fight or flight' responses are rarely appropriate in modern everyday life, and yet we can't easily turn them off. So what we need to do is pause before rushing to embrace them. We need to examine them and make a decision whether to accept or ignore them.

> *Don't allow yourself to be dazed by the speed of its impact, but say, 'Wait for me, impression, let me see what you are, and what you're an impression of; let me test you out.'*
>
> Epictetus, *Discourses* 2.18.24

The first step, then, is to slow down before rushing into judgement or action. We need to develop the habit of examining the first thoughts that come into our minds and interrogating them based on Stoic principles. Those first thoughts often include unconscious value judgements. We need to strip them out, so that we can get back to the experience itself.

> *Do not say more to yourself than first impressions report. You have been told that someone speaks badly of you. This is what you have been told; you have not been told that you have been injured … Always abide by first impressions and add nothing of your own from within.*
>
> Marcus Aurelius, *Meditations* 8.49

## Stage 2: Is this virtuous?

The next step in the process is to test our first thoughts to see if they are in conflict with what we deem to be good, virtuous behaviour. One nice example that Cicero gives is this: consider what you are inclined to do and ask yourself if this is something you would be willing to say or do in public.[34] If you feel the need to conceal an action, then it is probably not the right thing to do. If you would feel embarrassed to admit to it, don't do it! If you fear legal consequences, definitely don't do it! This can be one easy way to rule out certain courses of action.

There's another way that takes us back to Epictetus' ideas about what we do and don't control. Some things are 'up to us' and some things are not. The things that are in our control are – you will remember – all internal to us: our judgements and beliefs and actions. These are all closely associated with virtue, which is also an internal frame of mind. Everything else that is outside of us is beyond our full control. We can use this distinction as another guide. For instance, are you about to make a decision because you think it will earn praise and admiration from other people? If so, it might not be the right thing to do, because external praise is not 'up to us' and so in no way related to a virtuous character. Therefore, it ought to be of no consequence, and valuing it might lead us in the wrong direction. Don't do what other people might praise; instead, do what you genuinely think is the right, proper thing to do. If other people recognize that, they may well praise you for it, but whether they do or not is far less important than doing the right thing.

## Stage 3: The right thing

Having ruled out obviously misguided paths, there's still the question of working out what to do. The Stoics suggest there are two sets of principles we ought to keep in mind when deciding what to do. The first set are what we might call 'big picture' principles:

---

- ▶ We are all social animals and part of a single community.
- ▶ We are all part of Nature and rely upon it.
- ▶ Our individual benefit aligns with the common benefit.

---

These three closely inter-related ideas come up in all the Stoic texts; they are especially prominent in the *Meditations* of Marcus Aurelius. Throughout the *Meditations*, Marcus uses these guiding principles to help him decide what to do. Is he acting selfishly or for the common good? Is he treating other people as fellow citizens and collaborators or as opponents? Is he acting in a way that damages Nature, the source of all the things he needs in order to survive? It is by asking himself these questions that Marcus guides his own decision-making process.

> *If you have ever seen a dismembered hand or foot or a head cut off, lying somewhere apart from the rest of the body, you have an image of what a man makes of himself ... when he cuts himself off or when he acts anti-socially.*
>
> Marcus Aurelius, *Meditations* 8.34

Alongside these big-picture principles are others that relate to the specifics of our lives. We can call these 'role' principles. Each of us occupies a series of roles in life, some of which we have chosen (our job, for instance) and others that we have not (being a daughter, son, sister or brother). All of these roles come with certain expectations. Some of these might seem to be natural and universal (a parent's responsibility for their child), while others seem to be socially conditioned (the duties that come with a job). The Stoics say that these roles also give us a guide as to what we ought to do.

Epictetus gives the example of a judge.[35] Someone who voluntarily takes on the position of a magistrate also takes on the duties and responsibilities that come with such an important role. While we would hope that everyone treats others fairly and impartially, we expect it all the more from people in positions of authority. The same goes for a doctor. We expect high standards from people who take on such roles. The Stoics suggest that we ought to think about the different roles that we occupy and use them to help decide what would and would not be the appropriate thing to do in any given situation. If you occupy a leadership role, think about what would and would not be appropriate ways to behave for someone in that role. In light of what we have just seen in Stage 2, this isn't about what other people might think of us but instead what is the proper or appropriate way to behave. Thinking about the different roles we occupy can be one useful way to determine that.

Sometimes the different roles we have might lead to conflicting responsibilities. How do you balance your responsibilities as a parent or a partner with those of your job and career? There is no easy answer to this and each situation will be different, depending in part on how much value you place on each. Sometimes, specific 'role' principles might seem to come into conflict with big-picture principles. It is notable that Marcus Aurelius seems to suggest that big-picture principles should always come first.

> *As [Marcus Aurelius] Antoninus, my city and fatherland is Rome; as a human being, it is the cosmos. What brings benefits to these is the sole good for me.*
>
> Marcus Aurelius, *Meditations* 6.44

Chapter 12

# MEDITATIONS ON DECISION-MAKING

## JUSTIN STEAD

> *Your mind will be like its habitual thoughts;*
> *for the soul becomes dyed with the colour of its thoughts.*
>
> Marcus Aurelius, *Meditations* 5.16

Marcus Aurelius gets top billing from the ancient period as the most famous Stoic. As previously discussed, his rise to chair and CEO of the Roman Empire was a well-orchestrated and carefully nurtured process. Emperor Hadrian made the call for Marcus to be his successor, noting Marcus' brilliance as a young boy and ensuring his pathway to power through the adoption of Antoninus Pius, who became a segue emperor and mentored Marcus to the throne. It was a succession plan with real vision combined with careful, detailed management. He was determined to be Stoic but also determined to fulfil his duty as a productive and positive emperor and to ensure he 'did not spill any senatorial blood' during his reign.

That said, Marcus always made his decisions from the very top of the power totem pole, and this is a very different dynamic compared to being on a board or a member of a C-suite team. He was clearly thoughtful, deliberate, patient and considered in his words, decisions and judgements. We can see this in the *Meditations* but also understand it from reading his detailed legal decision briefs and his personal letters to his teacher Fronto.

Developing a decision-making framework through the Stoic lens takes time and is a process based on habits and discipline. Marcus Aurelius is an excellent example of developing a Stoic decision-making framework. Cicero and Seneca, on the other hand, although more prolific in their writings, come across as more flawed human beings, making decisions within immense power forums.

## Cicero: Weak convictions and decision-making lead to a death sentence

For the avoidance of doubt, Cicero is not known as a Stoic but he wrote about Stoic themes periodically and was certainly aware of the Stoics in Rome. I call him out in this chapter as someone on the same level of political power as Seneca, albeit living in a period well before Seneca and Marcus Aurelius. Cicero could have used Stoicism as an effective management tool to further his career, contribute to the greater good of Rome, and ultimately, to save himself.

Both Cicero and Seneca were brilliant men of their period, living in an incredibly dynamic but violent time. The sword, on a day-to-day basis, was mightier than the pen. However, I find them lacking in their decision-making when it really counted: they were conflicted between their desire for power, influence and material gain, versus staying true to the deepest Stoic values. Cicero met an untimely death during the proscription period of Augustus and Mark Antony's rise to power. Mark Antony had an intense dislike for him after Cicero had continually attacked him and his character, culminating in the writing of the *Philippics*, a series of speeches condemning Mark Antony. Augustus is alleged to have tried to keep Cicero off the proscription list, but Mark Antony was adamant.

This was a tough decision for Augustus: save the greatest orator, lawyer, philosopher and senator of the day, or sacrifice him for the current stability of the entire Roman Empire by placating Mark Antony, a partner he didn't like on any level but someone he had to do business with to ensure future progress and success. Augustus, no Stoic, chose stability at Cicero's expense.

The issue I have with Cicero, as a senior executive within the Senate, is that he could not commit himself to either side of the conflict using Stoic values. He prevaricated continuously during this period, all the way back to his interactions and relationship with Julius Caesar. He kept wavering between the Republicans (Brutus and Cassius) and the Imperialists (Julius Caesar and Augustus). Seemingly, he would play the middle ground and wait for the wind to change – good politics perhaps, but a lack of conviction led to his ultimate demise at the hands of Antony.

Stoic principles could have guided him to better partnerships or clarity over time. If he had taken a stronger Stoic stance, even standing beside Julius Caesar for the greater good of the Roman Empire, his fortune may have been different. He could have made a pragmatic Stoic decision: imperialism is wrong, but it is inevitably coming, and I will work within that system for the greater good. He tried to have his cake and eat it too, and it cost him his life.

## Seneca: Power corrupts, and absolute power corrupts absolutely

Emperor Nero ranks in the top three worst emperors in the history of Imperial Rome. Competition is fierce for this title considering Caligula (delusional and cruel), Commodus (ironically, Marcus Aurelius' son, but overly fond of excess and executions) and Caracalla (a brutal tyrant who assassinated his own brother) among others. Having to work within Nero's court must have been very challenging for Seneca, one of the most famous and acknowledged Stoic philosophers. I read his writings every day, and his command of language and his Stoic beliefs are remarkable, but his decision-making continuously seems adrift of true Stoic values.

His senior executive mentorship and influence over Nero waned dramatically over time, and he had to have witnessed, facilitated or confirmed numerous horrific acts of debauchery, violence and murder (including Nero killing his own mother, Agrippina). I must wonder: where did his stronger Stoic beliefs stand in this madness? And all the while, Seneca was assumed to be the second richest man in Rome. Seneca was likely the benefactor of estates and property of murdered senators and peers during Nero's reign. Seneca, very normal for his time, was an extremely ambitious person. But perhaps his ambition led him astray. In my opinion, of all the great Stoics, Seneca's executive decision-making distances his actual life from his Stoic philosophy the most. He reminds me of the saying, 'Do what I say, not what I do.'

I really have to question Seneca as the COO of the Roman Empire in what he did, observed and allowed to happen in his executive role. However, when I have put this opinion to John in the past, he makes an excellent point countering my position: Stoics were better off trying to stay within the system as powerful influencers. Although this would be challenging from a Stoic perspective, they could from time to time influence and help make better decisions for the greater good. If they were not there, arguably, things could have been even worse. At the end of Nero's reign, I am not sure it could have been any worse for those around Nero or the Empire's strategic and economic direction.

Cicero and Seneca were brilliant philosophers and writers, but ultimately flawed human beings whose desire for power and influence brought them both to early and brutal ends based on decisions that I would suggest were far from the deepest Stoic values. Where was the Stoic armoury when they needed it most? Their inability to stay consistent to the questions of 'Is this wise?', 'Is this just?', 'Is this temperate?', 'Is this courageous?' would prove to be very costly.

## CEO decision-making and accountability

The CEO of any organization is ultimately accountable for the performance of the business and what happens within it. For me, this accountability is two-fold: first, the professional execution of the business, and second, how I conduct myself and lead the team based on the values that define our culture. Over the years, I learned that decision-making from the CEO office became more nuanced if my strategy, tactical and financial work was done well upfront, and refreshed each year based on progress from the previous year. Crucially, the careful selection of the right people and management of the team to execute the agreed-upon strategy reduced the day-to-day decision-making as CEO.

Currently as chair across multiple enterprises, I do not make executive decisions on a daily basis – that is the role of the CEO. That said, I have a system of planning that is universal across most of my enterprises. My steps for lightening the decision-making load to create more clarity for all within the business are as follows:

- **Vision:** Create an exciting goal for the enterprise.
- **Strategy:** Formulate four to six fundamental strategic pillars to deliver the vision.
- **Tactical execution:** Create three to five actions or initiatives with clear milestones under each strategic pillar.
- **Financial plans:** Create extensive financial plans (P&L, balance sheet, cash flows) that make the vision, strategy and tactical execution possible.
- **Team structure:** Develop a team to execute the strategy. Select people with world-class character and best-in-class professionals.
- **Culture:** Transform the culture of the business over time to be a place where people are trusted, respected and want to give their best every day. The Stoic values play heavily in this cultural transformation.
- **CEO/chair interventions:** Use your time and energy effectively to meet the needs of the business and the

team – in other words, get into the fray as needed and get out of the way just as much depending on progress toward strategic and financial goals.

---

I have had three major enterprises over a 25-year executive career. Two of them were exceedingly successful: very strong financial performance, personal satisfaction and strong culture – we had a lot of fun as a team. The third enterprise, which was a seven-year commitment, was not as successful, financially or personally.

If your career has a roughly 70 per cent success rate, then you are almost certain to have done well on most fronts. Much like Roger Federer – who famously won 80 per cent of his singles tennis matches but only 54 per cent of the individual points played – it is vital to capitalize on your periods of success, while minimizing the downside performance and risk in your weakest moments. The key is to be very aware of what period you are in.

Sometimes things happen to a business that are completely out of everyone's control, and the business simply fails or does not meet its potential. Consider any of the major macroeconomic disruptions of the past twenty years. These so-called 'black swan' events destroyed businesses worldwide on an incredible scale, despite significant governmental intervention to protect businesses with direct financial support and low-cost loans. During these tough downside periods, you need professional excellence to survive but, just as much, a personal management system of resilience and an approach to handle problems ethically and morally.

## The private equity arena – ruthless but real

The private equity world is complicated and at times ruthless. Investors (equity), banking financial partners (debt), and management (execution) all walking a very thin tightrope together to achieve business and financial success. They battle for collective success but also, especially when things go wrong, mark their own zones of protection and defence.

The private equity model, as we know it today, has come under much scrutiny since its inception in the 1980s with leveraged buyouts. It can be a very lucrative game but also a cut-throat one. Financial performance is the bottom line, and the best private equity funds generate incredible returns for their investors. Competition is fierce among private equity firms to attract capital, and this capital will move to the best-performing groups – it is the law of the jungle.

CEOs, whether in private or public arenas, have a lot of complicated situations, constituents and expectations to manage. That is why the compensation is outstanding when success is achieved, but it comes with significant personal cost, time commitment and, if not carefully managed, wellbeing sacrifice. Like Marcus, Cicero and Seneca in their forums, there is a lot at stake for many collective interests but also for the individuals who play this game. Ensuring that good and consistent ethical decision-making is happening can be difficult, particularly when the economics turn south.

## Pinch points of conflict in decision-making

Having worked in and around private equity for over twenty years, with mixed success and failure, decision-making has not always been easy. I have had to balance investors' requirements and financial expectations with values that are very important to me as a person and as a Stoic. My boards and partners are generally very good at making decisions related to strategy, governance management, audit controls, capital deployment and banking. My biggest conflicts over the years with private equity partners and investors have been around *people* and *teams*.

In so many new ventures, the new investment group is excited about the business and the opportunity. They want to see their investment protected and a clear plan formulated. Once a plan is in place, the scrutiny turns to the team. The tendency is often to ensure every position within the team structure is 'perfect' to deliver results for that segment of the business – and this is where conflict has arisen. I have always been reluctant to make radical moves until there is enough time to see how people perform and adapt within a new management situation, team dynamic and company strategy. It takes time.

I can recall six distinct occasions when, after a board meeting, the shareholders and board asked me to fire certain C-suite executives and replace them accordingly. In each instance, I chose to stand against the chair and the board to save them. These firing requests were often impulsive and emotional, lacking bigger-picture understanding. However, I would always ask everyone to sit with their emotions for twenty-four hours and then discuss it again.

Personally, much to my chagrin, I have had to learn that impatience is a costly emotion, especially when it comes to managing people and difficult team decisions. Standing against your chair and the board to hold back the tidal request for a senior management exit is no easy task when you, as the CEO, know more than them when it comes to the value of the person; what they bring to the wider operating team; how they are viewed in the business; their experience and intellectual knowledge; and the cost to replace them in the commercial market.

## The Stoic decision layering process

Over the years, my framework as a committed Stoic has improved and become stronger through continual utilization of Stoic values and other Stoic frameworks across all decision-making, especially when big calls have had to be made.

My early CEO periods were marked with emotional reactions. It was not enough for me to just gain experience; I needed a stronger approach to improving my decision-making. I made many instinctual decisions around people to recruit, partnerships to back, costs to cut, investments to make and strategy to deploy around these tactics. Data and insights drive so much of business today across all segments, and this is a good thing for efficient working and confident capital deployment for shareholder returns. That said, as the years went on, I did not want to completely replace my emotions and instincts in my decisions. I wanted to utilize the experience that I was gaining, and I absolutely wanted to capitalize on data and turn numerical and quantitative insights into opportunities. But my strongest Stoic values were becoming more relevant on a day-to-day basis as I became chair across multiple enterprises, dealing with a host of different CEOs, investors, partners and consultants on a global business stage.

I would break down my thought processes in a very disciplined way:

---

1. What is my gut telling me from instinct and intuition?

2. What is my experience telling me from all my successes and failures?

3. What does the data reveal about what has happened and what could happen?

4. How does this decision sit with my Stoic values?

---

## Using Stoicism in CEO decision-making

During the 2020 Covid pandemic, the business I led needed immediate and emergency triage to save itself. Sales had collapsed, but all other expectations remained in place.

Therefore, decisive action had to be made on the cost and investment side of the business:

- Investments were immediately frozen or cancelled.
- All variable costs were reduced or cancelled.
- All sales-related costs were reduced or cancelled.
- And then the most difficult matter, a team review.

In a business where revenues had reduced by more than 50 per cent and sales channels had shifted significantly, we simply did not need the same structure or team of people to maintain the business for the foreseeable future. We had to make significant reductions and redundancies.

When I was looking at potentially a 50 per cent reduction in headcount across the business, I applied layers of Stoic thinking to support the final decision after going through steps one to three of my decision-making process above. These layers consisted of going through the cardinal virtues one by one:

- Is it **wise or just** to let so many people go during a pandemic?
- Is it **temperate** or balanced?

▷ Is it **courageous** to hold on to more people with less salary or make more decisive reductions?

▷ What is the best decision for *all* constituents within this situation: employees (future and potentially past), shareholders, suppliers, banks?

Taking all these points into consideration, I made the decision after careful work with the senior team and the board that the greater good and long-term security of the business, including employees that would remain at the business, must be protected. Difficult redundancies were made as soon as possible, and we held onto as many people as we could through assistance from the government furlough schemes. Obviously, many other CEOs came to a similar conclusion. But from a Stoic perspective, this example shows that bigger decisions can be underpinned by ethical values alongside clinical business analysis.

In the last decade, I have worked with partners and co-investors who wanted both: outstanding commercial leadership and a strong ethical code within our management team. The Stoic value system encourages management teams to think through the complete implications of their strategic, tactical and challenging decisions. Following all my decisions now, I challenge myself to answer these questions:

- Am I being wise, just, temperate and courageous?
- Am I thinking about the big picture, the view from above?
- Am I acting as a force for good, a part of nature, while being a good corporate citizen?

## Reflections on the Covid experience

The enterprise I led as CEO during the Covid pandemic will most likely not generate the return we were anticipating when we started the business in 2016. We had doubled profits from 2017 to 2019, and then the pandemic destroyed all those gains. We made the toughest decisions over a two-year period within massive dislocation. The outcome was that we protected the company, saved many jobs, grew the business in new markets away from the Covid destruction, and protected all our suppliers and banking partners.

Investor returns? We are still in that business and we will have to see how the final financial outcome will play out after a decade of effort. Sometimes just breaking even is a huge result considering what the business over a period of time had to endure.

Disappointing? Sure, in one sense. But in another, this was one of my best performances as a CEO, as we did not lose the company into administration or chapter 11 bankruptcy, or lose our total investment, which seemed the most likely outcome at one point.

Not everything in business is measured in money, and that was certainly the case for me during this period, working through tremendous stress, layering a Stoic mindset day after day to make decisions affecting people and families.

## The Stoic armoury

Applying Stoic virtues and values to your decision-making process, after rigorous business analysis, is a powerful ally to achieve success and contribute to the greater good. As Marcus wisely stated in Book 5 of the *Meditations*, 'Your mind will be like its habitual thoughts; for the soul becomes dyed with the colour of its thoughts.' As a CEO, dye your mind with questions concerning your actions before making big decisions – am I wise, just, temperate and rightly courageous? This approach builds confidence, independence and character, and allows for direct, confident communication within the boardroom – in good times but especially when things are tough.

By placing Stoic virtues at the heart of the decision-making process, the board knows the set of values the CEO is working from, which is not always apparent or known, especially when things are challenging. Such a CEO is clear in their conscience and sends the message that they cannot be bought for the wrong reasons. Most of all, a Stoic CEO can demonstrate that business can be a force for positivity in the world, doing great things that contribute strongly to the bottom line but also to the greater universal good.

## Summary & Reflection

- ▶ Marcus Aurelius stands out as a leader thanks to his excellent decision-making. Unlike Cicero and Seneca, whose brilliance was often undermined by ambition, inconsistency or fear, Marcus' decisions were measured, patient and ethical, grounded in virtue while navigating immense power and responsibility.

- ▶ For a modern CEO, leadership is about accountability, both in delivering results and in how you conduct yourself. Over time, I've learned to layer instinct, experience and data with Stoic values: asking whether each decision I make is wise, just, temperate and courageous.

- ▶ Regardless of the challenges you may be facing, the Stoic decision-making framework provides clarity and confidence, balancing ethical responsibility with practical outcomes. By embedding Stoic decision-making into daily leadership, CEOs can move from reactive firefighting to principled action.

Chapter 13

# REFLECTING ON TIME

## JOHN SELLARS

> *Life is long if you know how to use it.*
>
> Seneca, *On the Shortness of Life* 1.4

Our most precious resource is time. These days, it is all too common for people to complain that they are 'time poor', overstretched, with ever-increasing demands on their time and attention. The greatest challenge many of us face is staying focused on the things that matter most to us and avoiding the constant distractions that assault us from all directions.

Although this can often feel like a 21st-century problem – a product of the digital revolution of the past couple of decades – in fact it is nothing new. Stoics such as Seneca and Marcus Aurelius also struggled with, and reflected on, how best to manage their time. Their thoughts remain as relevant today as they were almost 2,000 years ago.

## Seneca on the value of time

Life is short. As the years pass, they seem to go by faster and faster. Just as you get into the stride of things, the journey is almost over. Life passes by so quickly that it is all too easy to miss it, lost in the busyness of endless, and often unrewarding, activity. Some people work and work and work, putting off the things that matter to them until retirement, only to drop dead from exhaustion before they can do any of them. This sounds like a modern story, but it is also what Seneca describes in his essay *On the Shortness of Life*. He describes the way in which some people in the ancient world used to complain that life is too short. But Seneca thinks that they – and we – are wrong to think that: 'it is not that we have a short space of time, but that we waste much of it'.[36] We have plenty of time, enough to achieve great things, so long as we make good use of it. We make our lives short by wasting so much of our time – unproductive meetings, unnecessary email traffic, addictive social media, endless rolling news. Seneca draws an analogy with money: a modest inheritance can go a long way if it is carefully managed and used effectively, but it can equally be frittered away on unnecessary indulgences and short-term pleasures, with nothing to show for it in the end. As a rule, people tend to be far more attentive to how they handle their money than to how they allocate their time. But time is far more valuable than money: it is always possible to earn more money, whereas time is a limited resource, always decreasing. Every moment counts.

Despite the fact that our time is an ever-decreasing resource, Seneca argues that if we learn to manage it properly there is no need to feel as if there is not enough. The distractions that he notes, writing in the first century AD, sound all too familiar:

- 'a toilsome devotion to tasks that are useless'
- 'besotted with wine'
- 'paralyzed by laziness'
- 'exhausted by ambition'
- 'driven on by greed across land and sea in hope of gain'

- ‘constantly dissatisfied, shifting from one new plan to the next’
- ‘with no fixed goal, simply pushed around by external circumstances’

We can no doubt all recognize examples of these issues in either our own lives or those of people around us. Evidently people in imperial Rome were not that different from us, which is why much of what Seneca has to say on this topic and many others still resonates today. No one in any of these states is really *living* in the fullest sense of the word. Too much of our existence is merely passing time, not truly being alive. This applies to both the lowest and the highest in society. The unfortunate are forced to work in unsatisfying roles simply in order to survive, while the successful face the pressures of managing their wealth and dealing with constant demands from others, to the point that they lose their own freedom. Everyone gives away their time to others until they have none left: ‘no one belongs to himself’.[37]

Having identified some of the distractions, Seneca goes on to offer solutions to improve our time management. First and foremost, we need to recognize that time is the most valuable commodity we have. We should think far more carefully about how we spend that than any other resource. Then we need to reflect carefully on what our goals are and what we are trying to achieve, ranking them in order of priority. We can then use that ranking to make sure that we only devote time to the things that matter most. It is not uncommon to meet people who claim that family is important to them, but who prioritize work so much that they rarely spend extended periods of quality time with their loved ones. Perhaps work *is* more important to them, which is their choice to make, or perhaps there's a mismatch between their values and how they allocate their time.

Indeed, perhaps unexpectedly, Seneca's central message when it comes to time management is not to try to become more efficient and get more done. On the contrary, he advises that we cut back on our commitments, limit the demands of others and slow down, so that we can actually enjoy the time we have, devoting it to the things that are most important to us. This should apply both at work and at home. He also warns against putting things off, especially those that matter most to us.

> *'After my fiftieth year, I shall retire into leisure; my sixtieth year shall release me from public duties.' What guarantee do you have that your life will last that long? ... Are you not ashamed to reserve for yourself only the remnant of life ...? How late it is to begin to live just when we must cease to exist!*
>
> Seneca, *On the Shortness of Life* 3.5

Are you continually putting off the things that matter most to you – whether that be in your personal life or in your career – to a hypothetical future that may never exist? As Seneca puts it, 'postponement is the greatest waste of life'.[38]

As well as this prioritization of goals, Seneca also warns against excessive busyness. It is easy to feel productive if one is constantly rushing around, but how much of the truly important work is actually getting done? To be busy with many things at once is to be distracted by many things, unable to focus on the task at hand. Seneca's advice is to do one thing at a time, slowly and deliberately.

> *No one pursuit can be successfully followed by someone who is busied with many things.*
>
> Seneca, *On the Shortness of Life* 7.3

In one striking observation, Seneca notes that people who are obsessed with longevity are often the worst culprits. They are the ones who are postponing their lives, hoping that by adding a few more years on the end they will finally have time to relax, enjoy themselves and do the things they really want to be doing. In contrast, those who are fully alive in the present, spending their time in effective and satisfying ways, are often far less concerned about how long they live, for they are living right now – quality over quantity.

## How many weeks?

Oliver Burkeman's book *Four Thousand Weeks: Time Management for Mortals* opens with a passage from Seneca's essay: 'This space that has been granted to us rushes by so speedily and so swiftly that all save a very few find life at an end just when they are getting ready to live.'[39] Both Burkeman and Seneca have the same aim: to jolt us out of our complacency by reminding us how little time we have. Burkeman's calculation of 4,000 weeks is his rough approximation of how many weeks we would have if we were to live to eighty years old. But, of course, there are no guarantees that we will live that long, and a significant number of people never make it to that age. Let's be blunt: if you end up with 4,000 weeks you've done well; your final tally may be a good deal less. According to the World Health Organization, average global life expectancy is around seventy-two years.[40] That's around 400 weeks less than if you were to reach eighty. And bear in mind that this is the *average*, which means that many of us may never reach that age. If 4,000 doesn't sound like many weeks, pause to reflect on how many people are unlikely to live anywhere near that long.

Let's be optimistic for a moment and assume that 4,000 weeks is within our reach. In fact, let's give ourselves a few extra, for eighty years is in fact 4,160 weeks. But how old are you now? How many weeks have you enjoyed already, never to be repeated? I write this around the time of my fifty-fourth birthday. I've already passed through some 2,800 weeks. Perhaps I'll have the chance to enjoy another 1,300 or so. But if my time ends closer to the WHO average expectancy I could have fewer than 1,000. Fewer than 1,000 weeks doesn't sound like very long at all. Even that is far from guaranteed.

## Only the present moment

One person who was all too conscious that there were no guarantees when it came to life expectancy was Marcus Aurelius. Marcus never knew his father, who had died in his early thirties when Marcus was just three years old. Later, Marcus and his wife, Faustina, had fourteen children together, many of whom died in infancy. We know of just four who made it to adulthood. Marcus lived in a world in which people were constantly reminded of their mortality, and his privileged position could not insulate him from this. In the *Meditations*, Marcus constantly reflects on his own mortality and how brief his own life was compared to the immensity of time. Rather than worry about how long he might have left, Marcus offers a highly practical solution: focus on what we have right now in front of us: the present moment.

*Practise only to live the life you are living, that is, the present, and then you will have it in your power at least to live out the time that is left until you die, untroubled and with kindness, reconciled to yourself.*

Marcus Aurelius, *Meditations* 12.3

There are multiple reasons behind Marcus' insistence that we ought to focus on the present moment:

1. Only the present moment exists. The past is gone and the future is not here yet: 'each of us lives only in the present, this brief moment; the rest is either a life that is past, or is in an uncertain future' (*Meditations* 3.10).

2. Neither the past nor the future is in our control. As we have already seen, the Stoics argue that there is no point wasting energy focusing on things we cannot control.

3. Dwelling on the past (regrets) or being overly concerned about the future (fear and anxiety) is likely to generate negative emotions that will limit our ability to think clearly and make good decisions.

4. The only way in which we can make a difference to anything is by acting in the here and now – in the present moment.

The problem is that we can become weighed down by over-analysing the past and excessively worrying about the future. What we need to do is bracket these off so we can focus on what needs to be done right now:

> *Do not allow the image of the whole of your life to confuse you, do not dwell on all the varied troubles that have come to pass and will come to pass, but ask yourself in regard to every present task: what is there here that cannot be borne and cannot be endured? You will be ashamed to admit it. Then remind yourself that it is not the future or the past that weighs heavy upon you, but always the present, and that this weight gradually grows less if you isolate it.*
>
> Marcus Aurelius, *Meditations* 8.36

So, Marcus recommends that we isolate the present moment, forget about what has already happened and cannot be changed, and avoid worrying about how things might turn out further down the line. What can be done right now to improve the current situation? That's the only thing within our control and that's the only way to make a difference. When feeling overwhelmed by too many problems and responsibilities, isolating the current task can be a useful technique.

Life is short and none of us know how long we have, but there is nothing we can do about that. What we can do is act right now, focusing our attention on the tasks and challenges immediately in front of us.

## Stoic time management

Pulling these threads together we can make the following points:

- ▶ Time is the most valuable resource we have because it is limited and cannot be replaced. It is worth dwelling on our own mortality occasionally to remind us of this fact.

- ▶ Given this, we ought to be very careful about how we allocate our time, only spending it on things that we judge to be the most important and valuable. We should be especially cautious about giving our time away to others on unnecessary, pointless or uninteresting tasks and projects.

- ▶ While learning from the past and planning for the future are important things to do, what matters is what we can do right now in the present moment. Let go of things that cannot be changed and do not be excessively invested in outcomes that cannot be known.

- ▶ Looking back to Antipater's archery analogy in Chapter 3, we ought to focus on the activity or the process, which is within our control, not the outcome or result, which is not. Time spent on an activity that is satisfying or inherently worthwhile is time well spent, regardless of the outcome.

# Chapter 14

# STOIC CEO TIME MANAGEMENT

## JUSTIN STEAD

> *You act like mortals in all that you fear, and like immortals in all that you desire.*
>
> Seneca, *On the Shortness of Life* 3.4

As I write this section on time management, we will naturally roll into other related matters for a Stoic – including the uncomfortable but essential topic of death. My personal schedule and life commitments currently consist of the following roles, responsibilities and professional endeavours, listed in order of importance and priority:

---

1. Evolving human being
2. Loving husband to my wonderful wife
3. Loving father to my cherished daughters
4. Loving son and brother to my immediate family
5. Loyal and committed friend to a short list of people – when they call, I answer immediately
6. Chairman, partner and investor to a portfolio of business interests
7. Founder of the Aurelius Foundation, our Stoic-led charity commitment for the next twenty-five years
8. Co-founder of the Rolling Stoics rock band
9. Other community advisory and role commitments
10. Tennis enthusiast always looking for the perfect game

---

As a Stoic, I undertake a continual auditing of my major activities and areas of focus every six months and therefore, the allocation of time to each area varies based on where it sits in my list of priorities – all things are not equal.

## Why?

In order to allocate my time effectively into the right areas of my life, I prioritize them clearly and agree on these priorities with myself (and with my wife).

Every six months, I review the major areas of my life to note any changes. From this discipline, anything outside this list that demands my time is generally a 'no' for me – a hard 'no'.

This list has changed, often dramatically, every three to five years or so as I have reached various life milestones and accomplished certain objectives, while also accommodating for failures and disappointments in not reaching some goals. This review process allows me to focus deeply on what matters most as the years proceed, both personally and professionally.

## Understanding concepts of time from the Greeks

The ancient Greeks had two distinct concepts of time: *chronos* and *kairos*.

*Chronos* refers to chronological or sequential time – the

measurable, quantifiable time of clocks and calendars. *Kairos*, on the other hand, signifies a qualitative, opportune moment – a fleeting window, seizing a moment when the 'time is right' for something.

Marcus and Seneca, as high-achieving executives and Stoics, would have been acutely aware of this distinction. In matters of people and society, they spoke in the mindset of *chronos*. When discussing personal growth and being Stoic, they spoke within the mindset of *kairos*.

Marcus is particularly obsessed with time, emphasizing how finite life is and urging us to start being great human beings now (*kairos*). Seneca focuses on using time well, insisting we have enough of it if we prioritize wisely (*chronos*).

As a CEO, one must carefully consider time in both ways. While *chronos* often gets the lion's share of attention to 'get things done', *kairos* cannot be neglected – it is essential for one's self-development to seize the moment with decisive action when inspiration strikes.

## The power of 'no'

The word 'no' is the secret to controlling your most important asset: your time. This asset becomes increasingly valuable as you move through the seasons of your life. Despite all the current excitement – dare I say hype? – around longevity science, the broad shape of how I see my life can be likened to the seasons:

- Spring: 0–20 years
- Summer: 20–40 years
- Autumn: 40–60 years
- Winter: 60+ years

As Stoics, we look at time and death more acutely and pragmatically than most. I am fifty-eight years old – the exact age Marcus Aurelius was when he died of the Antonine plague on the banks of the Danube. So, I must be honest with myself and take a close look at the time that I have left and how I spend it. We will all die – it is as natural a process as being born. Every creature and every human being who has ever lived has gone through this same process. We as Stoics are parts of Nature, we come from Nature and we will return to Nature.

## The evolving human being: Time management for yourself as a high priority

The top priority on my list is 'evolving human being'. Why? I dedicate significant time to my individual 'mind, body, spirit' improvement and wellbeing activities. I focus on what I can control: a great exercise regime, disciplined diet, daily meditation, limited alcohol, low sugar intake, daily fasting and a regular cold plunge and sauna routine. I believe that staying healthy provides a strong foundation for the rest of my life.

My biggest motivation to manage my time effectively is to spend as much quality time as possible with my three daughters. They are my world, despite Marcus' solemn Stoic warnings about the impermanence of loved ones.

## Knowing the ports: Know thyself as the Oracle of Delphi demands

Seneca reinforces this priority beautifully with his immortal maxim: 'If a man knows not to which port he sails, no wind is favourable.' I try to know all the 'ports' of my life so that the daily 'winds' of my energy and focus consistently carry me in the right direction. At fifty-eight, I feel I have the best handle yet on the great challenge from the Oracle of Delphi: 'Know thyself'.

I have outlined my current ports of destination and therefore need a strong combination of *chronos* and *kairos* time consideration to create a balanced and fulfilling human experience.

## Time management as a CEO

All these principles play out acutely in business as a CEO. The most successful CEOs are almost universally effective and productive, both for themselves and their teams.

In the late summer and early autumn seasons of my life, I became a CEO at forty. I was extremely well-travelled, had completed a strong education, and had significant global professional experience under my belt. I left the traditional corporate world to become a CEO in a private, more entrepreneurial company – a decision to focus on what the Stoics call an 'indifferent', otherwise known as money.

Now, I will be challenged on this as a Stoic. Both 'fortune' and 'money' are classified as 'indifferents', and I respect this principle greatly. Seneca talks so often about the fleeting nature of 'fortune and fame' and how fickle they are. Marcus is positively disdainful of fame and how silly it is to pursue it unnecessarily.

However, I valued the higher Stoic point on the value of time. My calculation was simple: the more financial independence I could create by my mid-autumn season (towards fifty), the more time I would have in the second half of my life – assuming I live to see all the seasons.

At forty, as CEO of a US$500 million turnover business, I was deeply conscious of using my time well. I have seen numerous colleagues perhaps misunderstand their seasons in life and how to manage their time within those seasons. Combine this with a lack of self-awareness, or clear goals and priorities, and it can be a recipe for personal disaster.

How many stressed-out leaders are trying to make it all happen at once? How many divorces do we see among executives? Given all the personal and professional priorities, each demanding a portion of your time, it's crucial for CEOs to set their priorities and plan their time accordingly. What are your personal and professional goals? Where do you want to allocate your time? Where do you need to allocate your time?

For me, I set my priorities rationally and clinically based on the season of my life. When I became a CEO at forty, my focus was on personal financial goals. I did not focus my time on finding a wife or starting a family at this point in my life – I knew that I could not divide my time between those responsibilities and my goals.

In a true *kairos* moment, I found the love of my life in the right moment, for which I am forever grateful.

## Eliminating the non-essential

It took me a while to find my feet and shift from a senior manager mindset to that of an effective CEO. My first hurdle was to stop being in too many meetings. Being everywhere only slowed things down, stifled better decision-making by my great executive team and undermined them.

I learned that I could be more effective by cutting down on meetings and putting in place a clear operational plan – vision, strategy, tactical plans, financial plans, capital structure, resource and team structure. That way, the entire operational platform and team would know what to do whether I was there or not.

On Mondays, we would check in on last week's performance. On Tuesdays, we would update on year-to-date progress while identifying opportunities and problems.

After Tuesday, I would work on strategic objectives across the business, major partner requirements or specific problems needing my direct attention. I didn't schedule meetings, but my teams knew I was available 24/7 for support, guidance or confirmation. My goal was to create a self-governing management system that encouraged and empowered leaders who were self-motivated and wanted to show their best work.

## Results and discipline

This approach worked excellently. From 2008 to 2012 at Aurum Holdings / Watches of Switzerland, we took profits from £6 million to £24 million, and the value of the business skyrocketed for shareholders. Best of all, we had an incredible time, winning year after year and making real changes in the luxury space.

We agreed on very disciplined time management protocols: most meetings were to be thirty minutes or less, every email or voicemail answered within twenty-four hours (even if not solved, then acknowledged). All meetings had a set agenda and focused strictly on the topic at hand. We made sure every meeting finished with everyone's needs met – not just ticking boxes or satisfying the loudest voices in the room.

We were on a roll, so we just kept moving. And as CEO, when the business has momentum, you need to get out of the way and get behind the team to reinforce the conditions that make success happen. Start the avalanche and then get behind and push more boulders downhill!

The finest example of this for me was Tom Kartsotis, the founder of Fossil Watch Group. Fossil is not the company it once was, but during its heyday it was remarkable. Tom was the ultimate entrepreneur: wise (hugely street smart), courageous (made huge calls only he could make to change dynamics), and just (incredibly fair with people). Temperate? Yes and no. The results during those years were extraordinary: billions in sales, healthy margins, global expansion and operating margins consistently above 15 per cent. And just as importantly, the team had a blast throughout. Now that is winning in business and in life – and it is rare. Tom was the heartbeat of the business, and he created momentum for a global team that loved what we did, how we did it and the results we achieved. Tom was a one in a billion entrepreneur and a person of the highest integrity.

## Seasons and sacrifice

The great chairman Don McCarthy inspired me to work harder, and for me it was the right 'season'. I had minimal family commitments and was focused on and committed to the business. I was willing to pay the price for success during this period.

Don was not a Greek scholar, but he understood the value of both *chronos* and *kairos*. He was the most efficient retail operator you could meet – brilliant and lucid, solving problems in ways others wouldn't consider. In one powerful luxury partner meeting, Don 'went off' at the principal CEO (my peer) over stock allocation. It was very uncomfortable. Afterwards,

I asked why. Don calmly replied, 'What is right is right, and we were right. Your friend, Justin, needs to know who stands behind you, and I like to use my time well with certain people to leave the right impression.' That partner never forgot Don.

Don also challenged me to do less, and at times nothing. 'Justin, doing nothing as a CEO is still actually doing something. Sometimes your inaction and letting things play out is more powerful than moving in too soon. Patience.' In our final years together, our status meetings were 25 per cent business and 75 per cent life. Our stage was set, and our roles and teams were outstanding. He showed me how to let the organization breathe once great people and structure were in place. Build the right channels and dams, and the water flows beautifully.

People sometimes suggested I was burning the candle at both ends during this period at Aurum / Watches of Switzerland. I was not. My priority list was different from the one on p. 173, as it was down to four primary things during that period: 1. health and wellbeing; 2. work and career; 3. core family and friends; and 4. social time and fun. Work was number two at this point because it aligned to my long-term goal: more time at a later date with my future family – at which time my priorities would change. Thankfully, my life has played out according to that plan.

## The coffee conversation

Perhaps the importance of spending your time strictly according to your priorities is best illustrated by a conversation I had with a talented young middle manager in 2010. He came to my office during 'coffee with the CEO', where anyone could come to see me for thirty minutes.

He said pointedly: 'I want to be like you. How do I do it? What's a plan or road map?'

I asked what he really meant by 'be like me'.

His response: 'I want the power, the influence, the money, and to drive a car like you.'

I said, 'Fair enough. But you do know it took me a while to get here?'

He replied, 'Oh yes, I get it, and I'm willing to do what it takes.'

I continued, 'Good. So, here's the plan: see you this Saturday at 9 a.m. until about 2 p.m. Bring lunch. Also, clear most weekends, certainly three out of every four, for the next few years. Devote this time to the business, become the best, and there will be no question of your promotion if you deliver.'

Saturday came, and I never saw him. Not that day, not any Saturday ever.

I don't judge him. It was an individual decision. For me, spending ten years in Dallas at Fossil and then at Watches of Switzerland working most Saturdays wasn't a sacrifice. I loved what I was doing. It wasn't time given up – it was an investment in my life, my career and my long-term goals. I was prepared to sacrifice this asset at that point in my life to accomplish things, in the hope that I would have to sacrifice less of it later in life. I wanted more of this asset when I believed it would count more for me. This was a personal decision and strategy for me and I am not suggesting it is right for anyone else – my Stoic approach and values formulated this plan for my specific objectives.

I knew my ports, I knew the winds I needed and I knew the time investment required – I knew the required sacrifice. These principles have not changed since time began, regardless of most endeavours for success.

The Stoics are clear and concise about time: how we should use it, what we should value, and when to use it well. Our lives are small and brief when compared to the incomprehensible age and size of the universe. But, as Seneca suggests, 'It is not that we have a short time to live, but that we waste a lot of it.'[41]

## Summary & Reflection

► Time is our most precious asset and managing it well is paramount to Stoics.

► I structure my life around a clear list of priorities, reviewing and adjusting it regularly. This disciplined focus allows me to say a hard 'no' to distractions and invest meaningfully in what matters most to me. As a CEO, this time management framework transformed me from simply being busy, to being *intentional*.

► As a leader and a person, your time is a finite and fleeting resource. You must respect it and invest it thoughtfully – for professional achievement, for your loved ones and for a fulfilling life.

Chapter 15

# THE BIG PICTURE

## JOHN SELLARS

> *A rational mind ... goes over the whole universe and the surrounding void and surveys its shape, reaches out into the boundless extent of time, embraces and ponders the periodic rebirth of the Whole and understands that those who come after us will behold nothing new and nor did those who came before us behold anything greater.*
>
> Marcus Aurelius, *Meditations* 11.1

What does it mean to be a leader? Among other things, it means taking overall responsibility for a project, group or organization. This requires stepping back from the everyday details in order to have a fuller, complete view of what is going on. Leaders who try to micromanage every detail of an operation rarely fare well, and part of good leadership is learning the art of delegation. The task of the leader is to comprehend the big picture.

## The view from above

No one understood this better than Marcus Aurelius. As Roman Emperor he was responsible for managing a vast territory spanning Europe, north Africa and Asia Minor. In order to comprehend the scale of what had been entrusted to him, Marcus often adopted what has been called the 'view from above'.[42] This practice involves breaking free of our usual first-person perspective on the world (so far as we can) and adopting a third-person perspective on the same situation, usually from a higher vantage point.

Consider the following example. Imagine you have an urgent appointment to attend, but you are stuck in traffic. All these other people are in front of you and *in your way*. You are trying to get somewhere, and *they are the problem*. Inevitably, the situation is frustrating, and you might start to get angry. But what if you could adopt a slightly different perspective on the situation. There is traffic. It is rush hour in a busy city – this is entirely normal and ought to be expected. Indeed, it would be unrealistic to expect anything else. As you imagine looking down on the situation from above, you can see that your car is one of hundreds queuing bumper to bumper. You are *part of the traffic*, and as much a part of the problem as anyone else, blocking people behind you, just as the cars in front are blocking you. Zooming out even further, you can imagine the same situation playing out in every major city in the country, every working day. It would be absurd to get angry about something so common and predictable as a traffic jam in rush hour. And it would be irrational to expect anything else.

Marcus used this technique to help him deal with everyday frustrations and difficulties in his role as emperor.

> *Watch and see the courses of the stars as if you ran with them. Continually dwell in your mind upon the changes of the elements into one another. These imaginations wash away the foulness of life on the ground.*
>
> Marcus Aurelius, *Meditations* 7.47

By looking at events from this higher perspective, Marcus was able to stop himself getting annoyed by everyday challenges and setbacks. It also prevented him from falling into egotism. Being ruler of the Roman world must have been the ultimate ego trip, and any leadership role comes with a similar risk. By adopting a view from above, Marcus could reflect on the fact that great figures from the past were now long dead, a few still remembered, but most quickly forgotten.

> *How many whose praises have been loudly sung are now committed to oblivion: how many who sang their praises are long ago departed.*
>
> Marcus Aurelius *Meditations* 7.6

So, this technique enabled Marcus to keep his ego in check, to remind himself of his own mortality and to put everyday setbacks into a bigger context, enabling him to avoid anger and frustration. But it also enabled him to see something else.

## Interconnectedness

One of the central themes and great insights in Marcus' *Meditations* is the idea that Nature is a single interdependent unity of which we are all parts.

> *All things are woven together and the common bond is sacred, and scarcely one thing is foreign to another, for they have been arranged together in their places and together make the same cosmos.*
>
> Marcus Aurelius, *Meditations* 7.9

This was a standard Stoic idea, dating back to the first Stoics in Athens. They saw Nature as a single organic entity – a living being – governed by reason. They insisted that there is order and structure within Nature, which does not act at random. Indeed, the fact that science is possible is precisely because there is order and regularity in how Nature works, enabling us to model it and to predict what will happen next. These topics are less relevant to our concerns here, but the idea that Nature is an integrated unity was especially important to Marcus. It crops up again and again in the *Meditations*.

> *I am part of the Whole which is governed by Nature ... I am allied in some way to the parts that are of the same kind with me ...*
>
> Marcus Aurelius, *Meditations* 10.6

## THE BIG PICTURE

There are a number of key ideas that we can take from this:

- Each of us is part of something larger than us.
- Our interests are aligned with the best interests of this larger thing.
- Whatever happens, if it benefits the larger thing, we should welcome it as benefitting us too.
- Everyone who is part of this larger thing should be working together for its benefit, which is the common good.
- To fight against other parts of the larger thing is ultimately against both the common good and our own self-interest.

There are important reasons to see ourselves as parts of a larger whole. Our wellbeing and indeed our very survival depend on the wellbeing of Nature. As parts of Nature, we are completely reliant on it for food, water, oxygen and everything else we need in order to live. As a consequence, it is in our best interest to see ourselves as integrated parts of Nature and to look after Her as best we can – being environmentally conscious, conserving natural resources, being responsible consumers and manufacturers. Not embracing this view could be fatal for us and for future generations.

Seeing ourselves as parts of the universe or Nature as a whole is the broadest perspective we can take. We might also see ourselves as parts of a wide range of other entities: parts of a single global community of humankind all working together; citizens of the county in which we live; colleagues within a company working to a common goal, and so on. In each case, by seeing ourselves as parts, we can feel more motivated to contribute to a common good that will benefit not only the whole but all the parts, including ourselves.

## Everything changes

Adopting the view from above, Marcus saw not only the interconnectedness of Nature, but also that Nature never stands still, not even for a moment. The world is in constant change, life is a process, things are continually growing but also dying. Life and death, birth and destruction, the cyclical patterns of the seasons – these are what we see when we step back and pause to contemplate the world around us from a higher vantage point.

> *There is a kind of river of things passing into existence, and time is a violent torrent. For no sooner is each seen, than it is carried away, and another is being carried by, and that, too, will be carried away.*
>
> Marcus Aurelius, *Meditations* 4.43

Marcus used this perspective on the world to manage his emotions when he faced change and loss in his own life. Every time something is born, he reminds himself, something else must die in order to make room for it.[43] If resources are to be deployed in a new project, inevitably they cannot be used somewhere else. Nature is a zero-sum game. In order to be able to see this – to have a sense of the large-scale development of something and how growth in one area might involve or even require decline in another – one needs to adopt the view from above. The lesson that Marcus draws from this is that nothing is destined to last forever. No living being can escape its ultimate dissolution and the same applies to everything else – families, companies, countries. Not even the Roman Empire could escape the natural end of its life.

## Stoicism for organizations

Marcus Aurelius was looking at the really big picture – at Nature as a whole and the meaning of life and death. The 'view from above' can be applied to a variety of contexts though, from small businesses to large corporations. Taking his insights on board, we can say:

▸ Any organization can be viewed as a single organic entity in which all the parts contribute to the success of the organization as a whole.

- All the parts 'play a role' and contribute something useful. No one part is more important than any other. The CEO and the security guard on the front door both have their jobs to do and make a contribution.

- Sometimes, for the organization to survive, some parts that no longer serve a useful function might need to go. While this is difficult for those involved, the big picture perspective will always ask what is best for the organization, not for any individual member, including the CEO.

- Anyone who pursues their own self-interest over the success of the organization has failed to see that their own flourishing depends on the success of the organization as a whole.

- Nothing lasts forever, not even large corporations. Most businesses close at some point. Few last through multiple generations. Those that survive for any length of time often go through dramatic transformations in order to survive. The physical, social and economic environment in which we live is constantly changing, and so we should expect to do so too – adapt or die, two forms of change.

Chapter 16

# A STRATEGIC VIEW FROM ABOVE

## JUSTIN STEAD

> *How tiny a fragment of boundless and abysmal time has been appointed to each man! ... And on how tiny a clod of the whole Earth do you crawl!*
>
> Marcus Aurelius, *Meditations* 12.32

The CEO role is the ultimate seat of accountability in any business. When things go well, the CEO is celebrated. When they don't, criticism is fast, direct and sometimes deeply personal. Many aspire to this role for the visibility, influence and financial rewards. But as a Stoic, I've come to understand these as 'indifferents' – external things that neither define nor sustain a worthy life looking out from the inner citadel.

When I first became a CEO, I discovered a sobering truth: the external accolades are fleeting, but the internal pressure is enduring. The weight of strategic decisions, cultural influence and operational consequence became immediately clear. Without discipline, the noise of daily operations could quickly derail the strategic vision I was hired to deliver.

In those early months, I made the classic mistake of acting like a senior operator rather than a strategic executive. I was trying to manage every function – marketing, finance, logistics – despite having highly capable C-suite partners. My leadership was hampered by my instinct to control rather than to trust and lead.

## The Stoic shift: Leading strategically

Two major Stoic adjustments changed my leadership trajectory:

1. Let nature take its course – through a clear and credible strategy. My role was to ensure the strategy was right, believed in and repeatable – then consistently deliver it, without stepping into operational roles that belonged to others.

2. Be in the right conversations, not every conversation. I had to overcome the urge for immediate validation and shift toward longer-term value creation. My job wasn't to be omnipresent, but omni purposeful – to remove roadblocks, reallocate resources and reinforce mission clarity.

The most powerful catalyst for this transformation was the Stoic principle of the 'view from above' (see Chapter 15).

## The view from above: The essential Stoic leadership lens

The Stoics taught that by mentally rising above one's immediate concerns and seeing life from a higher vantage point, we gain clarity, emotional control and philosophical calm. Marcus Aurelius often imagined looking at his life from the stars, shrinking problems down to their true scale. As a CEO, this became an indispensable practice.

## CASE STUDY 1: LUXURY BRAND NEGOTIATIONS (2007)

In 2007, I took over a respected but fatigued UK luxury business. It had rich heritage and smart executives – but lacked a strategic engine, coherent customer engagement and true brand partnerships. Our goal was a five-year turnaround.

One of the most radical actions I took early on was renegotiating terms with nearly every luxury brand partner within a thirty- to sixty-day window. It was bold, necessary and, as I quickly discovered, controversial. The Friday after our new terms and proposal letters went out to all partners at once, my phone exploded with hostile messages – from London to Geneva to Paris. Accusations flew thick and fast: 'you're out of your depth', 'who do you think you are?' Some even suggested that I resign.

So, I did what Stoicism had trained me for: I didn't react. Instead, the weekend after the negotiations kicked off across the entire partner base, I flew to Inverness and walked into the Scottish Highlands, turned off my notifications and metaphorically climbed to the moon. From this 'view from above', I saw the bruised egos, the turbulence and unrest I was causing, the potential impact on myself and my job – but also the long-term necessity for the business. The easy option would have been to drop negotiations, but the right option was to persevere. I let the emotion pass through me, anchored myself and prepared to calmly and methodically respond the following week.

We held our line. Over time, we rebuilt partnerships on stronger terms. Between 2008 and 2014, profits quadrupled. Everyone won. But only because I led from *above*, not from *within* the storm.

## CASE 2: MASS LAYOFFS – BALANCING DUTY WITH HUMANITY (2007 AND 2020)

Few situations test a leader's character like laying off employees. I faced this both during the 2007 financial crisis and again in the 2020 Covid pandemic. These weren't abstract 'headcount adjustments' – they were human lives. Families. Reputations. Futures. During these crises, the 'view from above' became my anchor. It helped me, not to suppress feeling but to act with clarity and composure. It reminded me: leadership is service, not popularity. I leaned into the four Stoic virtues to guide my decisions:

- **Justice** – I led the communication myself. No euphemisms. Just truth, delivered respectfully. Fair process, clear rationale and integrity in execution.

- **Wisdom** – I saw the broader implications. Saving the business meant saving hundreds of future jobs. The temporary pain, while profound, was essential for long-term preservation.

- **Courage** – I felt the anxiety, the personal guilt. But I stood up, faced the team and carried the message. Not with bravado, but with steadiness.

- **Temperance** – We didn't just meet legal obligations, we acted generously. Severance, outplacement and support weren't just line items. They were leadership choices.

—— A STRATEGIC VIEW FROM ABOVE ——

# Visualizing the perspective: A leader's elevation model

To illustrate the 'view from above', consider this layered model:

---

'The Higher You Rise, The Clearer You See'

### COSMIC PERSPECTIVE
'What truly matters?' Stoic clarity:
Legacy, Virtue, Duty

↑

### SOCIETAL IMPACT LAYER
Stakeholders | Economy | Industry | Brand ethos

↑

### ORGANIZATIONAL VIEW – SYSTEMS THINKING
Long-term strategy | Mission
Financial viability | Culture

↑

### HUMAN LAYER – INDIVIDUALS & TEAMS
Employee wellbeing | Team morale
Personal stories | Emotions

↑

### GROUND LEVEL – CEO EMOTION
Stress | Guilt | Pressure | Urgency | External noise

---

## Leadership with elevation

The 'view from above' is not detachment; it's discernment. It allows the CEO to lead without being overwhelmed, to act with integrity when under siege and to pursue the long-term good even when the short-term pain is great. Whether negotiating with global partners or showing leadership during layoffs, the ability to rise above immediate emotion and see the fuller picture has been my greatest advantage – not just as a leader, but as a human being. This Stoic lens has kept me steady, ethical and, ultimately, effective. Because when you lead from above, you lead from principle.

## Summary & Reflection

▶ As a CEO, your goal is not to be omnipresent, but omni purposeful. Your responsibility is to set a clear overall strategy and build a strong culture, not to oversee or step into every operational role.

▶ When you are faced with a difficult decision, try adopting the 'view from above' to gain clarity and perspective. Rising above the immediate noise will help you to fully appreciate the short- and long-term effects of your actions on everyone involved.

## A STRATEGIC VIEW FROM ABOVE

- ▶ Leading with the 'view from above' helped me learn when to engage, when to delegate, when to step back and when to stand firm. It anchored me in the four cardinal virtues – justice, wisdom, courage and temperance – so that even painful decisions could be carried out with fairness and humanity.

- ▶ To lead from above is to remain steady in crisis, principled under fire and devoted to the long-term good over short-term ease.

# Chapter 17

# NEXT STEPS

## JOHN SELLARS

> *No longer talk about what it means to be a good man; be one.*
>
> Marcus Aurelius, *Meditations* 10.16

Throughout this book, we've talked about the importance of developing character and cultivating the four virtues of justice, moderation, courage and wisdom. In practice, what does this mean? To say that someone is 'just' or 'fair' is simply to say they habitually behave in just and fair ways. They have developed the habit of making decisions based on certain values. Anyone can exercise moderation or courage in certain moments, but the challenge is to make this a deeply ingrained habit, so that you *consistently* act moderately and courageously.

## Epictetus on habits

How do we develop good habits? Habits are simply the consequence of acting in a certain way. If you want to develop the habit of reading, read. If you want to develop the habit of running, run.[44] There's no other way to do it. Equally, if you have a habit you want to break, you simply need to do the opposite. That might involve a period of complete avoidance, even if the ultimate goal is to reach a moderate middle ground. For example, someone who wants to cut back on alcohol consumption might struggle if they just resolve to drink a bit less. Only a complete break from drinking will help to break the habit. But once the habit is broken – unless there is a severe addiction – that doesn't mean abstinence for ever. Epictetus calls this developing 'contrary habits'.

> *What remedy can be found to use against a habit? The contrary habit ... counter a habit by setting a contrary habit against it.*
>
> Epictetus, *Discourses* 1.27.4–6

The sort of training Epictetus has in mind is less to do with diet, drinking or exercise, and more with how we think about things. His concern is with the negative patterns of thinking we develop, such as catastrophizing whenever something goes wrong, getting angry with other people or assuming that our plans will always go the way we want. The most dangerous habit that we all suffer from is rushing to judgement. As we have already seen, it is vital to slow down before making a judgement or decision in any situation, in order to avoid accepting a mistaken value judgement. So, the first and most important habit to cultivate is to slow down our thought process, to take our time before acting, creating the space to make calm and deliberate decisions. We can't effectively govern anything else if we can't govern our own minds.

## Virtuous and vicious circles

Habits are produced by actions. Every action contributes in some way. If someone wants to develop the habit of daily exercise, for instance, every time they manage to do some, that will contribute positively. If they do it once, they'll be more inclined to do it again, and after just a few times, a new habit has the potential to develop. Indeed, that's the *only way* a new habit can develop. Just a few good days can start to feed into a virtuous circle, where each success reinforces the new habit.

Equally, every time they don't do it, that will contribute negatively, and it is all too easy to fall into a vicious circle. Epictetus says that all actions are either good or bad in two ways:

> ▶ A good action is good but also has the further benefit of contributing to a good habit.

> ▶ A bad action is bad but brings with it the further danger of feeding a bad habit.[45]

In other words, the risks and rewards of an action are far greater than we might think. Epictetus says that because of this, we need to remain on guard at all times – on guard against our own minds and the minor slips that we might make, slips that can feed and breed dangerous habits. As we've seen, the most important thing is paying attention to our judgements. Every time we fail to do this, Epictetus warns, not only will we have made a mistake, but we'll also have contributed to a habit.[46] Epictetus' teacher Musonius Rufus once said 'to relax the mind is to lose it'.[47] The stakes are high! But the positive counterpart to this is that every small victory also comes with a further benefit of contributing to a positive habit, which can quickly snowball into real progress.

## Avoiding negative influences

In practice, life is far more complicated than this simple picture suggests because we are all constantly surrounded by external influences, which all too often shape the way we think and act. We are often influenced by the habits of the people around us, even if we are not conscious of it. If we are secure in our own beliefs and habits, then this is less of a problem, but if we are trying to develop new habits and break free of existing, unhelpful ones, this can make it even harder.

Epictetus reflected on this too. One of the key bits of advice he gave to his students was that they should be very careful when thinking about who they wanted to spend time with. As he puts it, if you spend time with people covered in dirt, you are likely to end up covered in dirt yourself.[48]

Imagine the following scenario. Two old friends enjoy meeting up regularly over a drink or two. One of them has decided for health reasons to cut back on their drinking; indeed, their doctor has advised them to give up alcohol altogether, at least for a while. The other friend has no such concerns and is happy to continue as before, with a firm belief that a good drink helps him unwind after a long day. When they next meet, one of them has a firm and secure habit about the benefits of a relaxing drink, while the other is trying to develop a new and far-from-embedded habit of not drinking. Which of the two is more likely to influence the other? Epictetus suggests that the new weaker habit is far more likely to be overwhelmed by the stronger existing habit than the other way round.

So, if you are trying to break a bad habit, the first thing to do is to avoid people who share that habit. That might be difficult and could involve severing some existing relationships. Equally, if you are trying to develop a good habit, an excellent strategy can be to spend time with people who already embody the qualities and skills that you want to develop. Choose your company well.

All this applies to someone in the early stages of trying to develop new habits. The goal, of course, is to have these habits fully embedded so that you are confident that you'll act in the way you want, no matter what the situation might be. The message is that we should be especially cautious when we are trying to make a change, while remembering that the result will be security and confidence to do the right thing no matter who we find ourselves with in the future.

## Consistency

Developing the right habits is the only way to develop character. A good character is one that *consistently* acts well. This idea of consistency is central to Stoic thinking and there are a number of different aspects to it:[49]

- ▸ Having a consistent set of beliefs and values that work together, not pulling in conflicting directions.

- ▸ Having consistency between what one says and what one does.

- ▸ Acting consistently over time, with the added benefits of being predictable, reliable and dependable.

We tend to admire people who are not internally conflicted, who do what they say and who can be relied upon. Inconsistency and unpredictability are not good character traits to have.

For the Stoics, the key to all of this is to be *rational*. The goal is to have a set of rational beliefs that, because they are rational, all fit together without contradiction. By slowing down our judgements, we can avoid unhelpful irrational emotions and make careful, thought-through decisions. This will help us to act in harmony with our beliefs and values, rather than getting distracted by outside influences or knee-jerk responses. If we can turn this into a habit, we'll develop consistency over time. People will come to know who we are and how we behave, in a way that is dependable and reassuring.

Chapter 18

# DAILY STOIC DISCIPLINES

## JUSTIN STEAD

> *Hour by hour resolve firmly to do what comes to hand with dignity, and with humanity, independence, and justice. Allow your mind freedom from all other considerations. This you can do, if you will approach each action as though it were your last, dismissing the desire to create an impression, the admiration of self, the discontent with your lot. See how little man needs to master, for his days to flow on in quietness and piety: he has but to observe these few counsels, and the gods will ask nothing more.*
>
> Marcus Aurelius, *Meditations* 2.5

## Daily Stoic disciplines:
## How to develop your 'inner citadel'

For many years, all over the world, in business settings and beyond, I have been speaking on, lecturing about, debating and discussing Stoicism with incredibly diverse audiences from all religions, ethnicities, genders and age groups. The idea that Stoicism is a force for good is generally accepted. However, there is always healthy debate on all matters around Stoicism, and I welcome this because, like any philosophy for good living, Stoicism should be tested generation after generation for its relevance and validity.

At a recent seminar hosted by the Aurelius Foundation at the University of Oxford, I was challenged on the benefit of Stoicism for a family trying to meet the demands of the cost-of-living crisis in East London, where starvation was a real problem. Another person asked about being made redundant again and the difficult challenge of finding permanent employment. Someone else challenged me on how Stoicism can help young people addicted to their phones and losing all sense of reality. These are all real problems in today's world, and they are serious issues for the people involved.

My response to these challenges is not lower-case stoicism with a 'stiff upper lip', hoping they will go away. The Stoicism that I practise does not avoid the problem or wish it away. Rather, it helps people, in whatever circumstance they find themselves, step into the day and into the arena. It gives them a system to work through problems profoundly and systematically, using the full Stoic toolkit.

Hunger pains won't be cured by Stoicism. But managing meal intake, understanding rationing and seeking support can be better approached with a Stoic mindset. The problem doesn't go away, but how we handle it is transformed. The same can be said about unemployment. Losing a job – especially repeatedly – can shake your sense of identity and self-worth to the core. It can feel as if the world has singled you out unfairly, leaving you without direction or dignity. Stoicism doesn't magically restore your employment, but it does give you a framework to navigate this painful reality and find employment again.

When I speak to people going through these struggles, I emphasize the principle of focusing on what is within our control and the 'view from above'. You cannot control the hiring decisions of others or the macroeconomic environment. But you can control how you prepare each day, how you show up in interviews, how you continue to build your skills and how you maintain your personal integrity.

Stoicism reminds us that our true worth is not defined by our current job title or bank balance. Our worth is measured by our character: our courage to keep moving forward, our ability to stay just and fair even in disappointment, our commitment to temperance when fear tempts us to act desperately, and our wisdom in seeing setbacks as part of the larger unfolding of life.

The Stoic mindset allows us to turn even periods of extreme difficulty into times of learning and strengthening – an opportunity to refine our 'inner citadel' so that when the next challenge arises, we meet it not as a defeated person, but as someone stronger and more self-aware.

## The process above all

There is always one question I consistently get asked after almost every presentation I give: 'How does one live like a Stoic?'

In other words, what are the daily things I do that allow me to maintain a Stoic mindset as well as I can – across all my different roles and experiences throughout the day: as a man, a husband, a father, a son, a sibling, a friend, a chairman, an investor, a tennis player and so on.

As in all ventures, the outcome is important, but even more important is the process. We've all heard the clichéd athletic reasoning: it's about the day-to-day experience of doing the work – the training and effort that allow someone to perform consistently over time and create opportunities for success.

Roger Federer has eloquently described his winning percentage as being lower than people think; my great friend Pat Cash, who lifted the Wimbledon trophy in 1987, also explains brilliantly the long journey of preparation that led to that defining moment. The same is true in my experience of managing large enterprises – the day-to-day process paves the way for success. Beyond my professional life, there is a personal set of disciplines that work for me every day – putting me into my 'best process' and 'calm self', not only to succeed in business but also to strengthen my character across all my daily roles and interactions.

## My daily Stoic practices

Here is my daily process – not as a prescription, but as an example of what works for me:

- **5.45 a.m.: Rise early** to embrace the day proactively.
- **Meditation (30 minutes):** Cultivate mindfulness and clarity.
- **Read Marcus Aurelius (5 minutes):** Internalize Stoic wisdom.
- **2-mile walk with dogs:** Connect with nature and reflect.
- **Physical exercise (30–45 minutes):** Strengthen body and mind.
- **Cold plunge (10 minutes):** Embrace discomfort to build resilience.
- **Lemon and hot water:** Simple nourishment to start the day.
- **Intermittent fasting (16–18 hours):** Discipline in consumption.
- **Midday reflection (5 minutes):** Assess alignment with virtues.
- **Evening journalling:** Reflect on actions and growth.
- **Reading Seneca before bed:** End the day with philosophical insights.
- **Virtue filter:** Continuously assess actions through the lenses of wisdom, justice, courage, and temperance.
- **No personal social media:** Maintain focus and mental clarity.

## A system unique to you

It is important to realize that these practices work for me, but I'm not suggesting they would work exactly the same for you or anyone else. Over many years, I've changed and revised them to build a daily Stoic foundation – working on my internal source of personal strength and harmony that I draw upon in every situation that arises. We work on our physical fitness, we work on our careers, we work on our relationships, but do we work on developing character, deep resilience and calmness daily?

I cannot control all the people, situations, problems or opportunities that appear every day in my life – but I can carry a system into each day that I cultivate, to build a Stoic shield of independence, optimism and calmness, no matter what happens.

My system works for me. Yours will be different and unique to you – but without question, building a system to manage your life is crucial. My daily process, deeply embedded in Stoicism, has been the foundation of my personal and professional life.

## Why discipline matters in leadership

What do people want most from those they choose to follow? In my experience working with exceptional businesspeople, it's two things: consistency and the ability to maintain calmness under pressure. Marcus Aurelius often speaks about consistency of character in the *Meditations*, and it remains one of my favourite Stoic principles.

# The daily Stoic process – Building your inner citadel

### THE INNER CITADEL
Calmness | Clarity | Strength | Resilience
(Core outcome)

↑

### DAILY VIRTUE FILTER
Wisdom | Justice | Courage | Temperance
(Guiding questions throughout the day)

↑

### CORE DAILY DISCIPLINES
- 5.45 a.m. rise
- Meditation (30 minutes)
- Read Marcus Aurelius
- 2-mile nature walk
- Physical exercise
- Cold plunge
- Intermittent fasting
- Midday reflection
- Evening journalling
- Seneca before bed
- No social media

↑

### PERSONAL ENVIRONMENT CHOICES
- Simplicity
- Mindful consumption
- Distraction-free spaces

Each layer reinforces the next, culminating in a resilient, virtuous and adaptable daily self.

Your daily disciplines are not simply habits – they are the foundational bricks and mortar of your inner citadel. Each layer fortifies your mind and character, empowering you to navigate life's challenges with dignity and strength.

## Life is not meant to be easy: Process to build character

Marcus puts it perfectly in *Meditations* 2.5 – the quote I opened this chapter with and one that I return to constantly. I sense in it the great disciplines that Marcus must have worked on daily to prepare for his many roles: emperor, husband, father, brother and friend. My process is not about rigidity or self-denial. It is about freedom. Freedom to respond, not to react. Freedom to remain steady amid storms. Freedom to act from principle rather than impulse.

I encourage you to build your own system – your own path to your inner citadel. And remember: the journey is uniquely yours.

## Summary & Reflection

- Living as a Stoic is not an abstract philosophy but a daily discipline.

- I create discipline by following a system of daily practices, which include exercise, meditation and reading Stoic works. Your practices might look very different to mine – the form the system takes isn't important, as long as it cultivates discipline to bring you closer to Stoic principles.

- Discipline is often misunderstood as rigidity but I see it as a path to freedom. True freedom is not found in ease or indulgence, but in the steady strength to respond with principle rather than react with impulse.

- Daily Stoic practices aren't about immediate perfection but about building an inner citadel brick by brick – a place of calm and clarity that sustains you through volatile or uncertain moments.

- Stoicism will not make the challenges in your life magically disappear, but it will give you a toolkit to face them with greater clarity, dignity and strength.

# Chapter 19
# FINAL REFLECTIONS

## JUSTIN STEAD

> *You will earn the respect of all if you begin by earning the respect of yourself.*
>
> Musonius Rufus, fr. 30

The core idea for the Aurelius Foundation came to me and my wife Natalia in my fiftieth year. We wanted to create an enterprise and a charity to which we could devote our time, resources and energy over a sustained period – in this case, at least twenty-five years, until I turn seventy-five, if I am granted that much time to live. It is easy to give money; it is much harder to give time. And if you are going to do both, the cause must be something to which you are, and will remain, deeply committed.

We have three beautiful daughters, so it was important that the Aurelius Foundation would, over time, become potentially meaningful to them as well. Every morning, when I drive my daughters to school, they read me a passage from the *Meditations*. Although they do not yet fully understand Marcus' meandering thoughts about life and the cosmos, they are beginning their Stoic journey as human beings within a philosophical framework that their parents deeply believe in.

Stoicism is not a religion, but rather an all-encompassing life management system with the goal of helping and enabling human beings to flourish whatever their circumstances. From the destroyed businessman Zeno, the founder of Stoicism, to the lowest slave in Epictetus, to the highest nobility of Marcus Aurelius as Roman Emperor – everyone has their problems, challenges and opportunities. The key is to live your life to the fullest and to take on all situations with the right attitude and approach as you work through countless circumstances in your own universe.

As a philosophy major for a time in college and a wandering seeker around the world in my youth – travelling with nothing but a few tennis racquets – I was deeply curious to answer one central question: *How do you live well?*

After travelling lots, including spending time in southern Japan exploring Buddhist and Zen temples, I kept coming back to Stoicism – mostly for its cultivation of deeper thinking and pragmatic, action-orientated approach to working through life's problems to create stong wellbeing and contentment. I came to realize that Rudyard Kipling's monumental inscription at the entrance to Centre Court at Wimbledon is correct:

> *If you can meet with Triumph and Disaster*
> *And treat those two imposters just the same*
>
> Rudyard Kipling, *If*

For a long time, I only saw the winning side of any situation as the answer and goal – how wrong I was.

## Stoicism, please find me earlier!

One of the Foundation's primary goals is to bring Stoicism to a younger audience as early as possible. Invariably, and perhaps unfortunately, most people come to Stoicism only after they have befallen a personal tragedy or life has come off the tracks. They need answers, recovery and light at the end of a dark tunnel – 'How do I get out of this hole and this mess?'

I recall Pat Cash asking me years ago, after reading the *Meditations*: 'Why is this not mandated for every child in school?' So many CEOs have said the same when they come to our seminars. Perhaps the most powerful voices for wanting to have known about Stoicism earlier in life come from the darker and more isolated corners of the UK prison system. The Aurelius Foundation's mission is for people in all walks of life and society to become aware of Stoic principles *before* the need for them – before life inevitably throws a curveball into normal existence.

## Stoic prison warriors

At His Majesty's Prison Huntercombe in Oxfordshire, England, there is one of the most important Stoic hubs in the world. This Stoic programme is moving forward quietly but with assured momentum, making a profound difference in many lives. Boris Becker, one of the greatest tennis players ever and a global celebrity, can directly attest to this because he was profoundly transformed by the Stoics at Huntercombe.

Since 2017, Andrew Small, a prison education officer, with the backing of his visionary governor David Redhouse, has created, refined and implemented a Stoic training course for prison inmates at Huntercombe. Andy came to Stoicism following the devastating suicide of a best friend who seemingly had it all in life. Andy needed more answers to this tragic situation, and it was Stoicism that helped his journey of understanding and acceptance of his friend's passing.

The programme is a sixteen-session course introducing deep Stoic education and training. The Aurelius Foundation supports this initiative at Huntercombe and across seventeen other prisons throughout the UK, and as far afield as the Falkland Islands. Our goal is to implement this Stoic programme in all UK prisons, and eventually across global prison systems. The programme has resulted in reduced aggression and violence inside Huntercombe. It's important when celebrities, great leaders and sporting champions reference their Stoic credentials. But when you are a prisoner, locked in a cell 24/7, that is hardcore Stoicism being lived, every second.

Stoicism does not look to change that reality or sugarcoat any situation. These prisoners realize, through their Stoic course of understanding, that this is the time to recognize past mistakes and learn from them. They work through the following process:

---

▶ Understand that this is my reality for the foreseeable future.

▶ Realize and accept how long I am going to be here.

▶ Accept why I landed here and that it was ultimately on me.

▶ Formulate how I can turn this incarcerated time to my advantage.

▶ Make significant changes so I do not end up here again.

---

—— FINAL REFLECTIONS ——

These are tough self-reflections and hard-hitting realities. Yet, the graduates of this course do change, and I have witnessed firsthand the dramatic results Stoicism has delivered.

## A Stoic prisoner's journey

Jay Adam is a native Somalian who came to the UK with his family to escape war and famine in the late 1990s. It remains deeply challenging for immigrants to come to the UK and not be properly integrated into society. Jay and his extended family lived in a Somalian community in East London – a world unto themselves. Without proper support, the negative influences on Jay were extreme.

Pressured by the need to provide for his family, Jay headed down a path of selling drugs to create income, to be the provider and to gain status for himself. At one point, he was a leading figure in the home counties drug scene, with tens of thousands of pounds of illicit trades running through his network every day. It was a significant business and very profitable – for a time.

Eventually, the situation spiralled out of control and the law finally caught up with Jay – twice. He was sentenced two times, with the second stint landing him in Huntercombe Prison. It was there that he encountered Andy Small and thus began an extraordinary friendship and a journey of self-transformation, starting with the ultimate question all Stoics must answer: *What is your purpose?*

This question often becomes the most telling and profound moment for people when they hit rock-bottom – the moment someone crosses the 'razor's edge' into greater self-understanding. People either submit to their circumstances and seek truth, or they continue to blame the world and others for their predicament. They keep kidding themselves, and never learn the real truth about themselves.

In Jay's case, when Andy Small looked him in the eye during his first Stoic session and demanded an answer, Jay was at a loss for words. 'What is my purpose? What is my purpose? What is my purpose?' The question echoed in his mind for days. He wanted not only to answer it but to learn everything he could about the source of that question.

I have seen Jay give many presentations over the years to audiences searching for the same answer: *What is my purpose?* I have had the great privilege to get to know Jay deeply, and this question is always central in his talks – whether at the University of Oxford, local football clubs in London or in intimate workshops.

The most incredible moment for me was seeing Jay speak to 150 CEOs and their partners in April 2024 at the Academy of Athens – the intellectual heart of Greece. As he looked out at this group of CEOs and very successful people, they were completely enthralled by his Stoic journey and his mastery of the subject as a modern-day Stoic philosopher. You could hear a pin drop at one of the most important centres of learning in the world – the home of the Greek intellectual immortals!

Not half a mile away, Zeno himself had founded Stoicism, and I am certain Zeno would have been proud of Jay's articulation to this audience. He paused at the start of his presentation just to take it all in. It had to be a mind-blowing moment – just a few years before, he was locked up in Oxfordshire facing four years and deportation. His ticket out of that disaster was provided by Andy Small, his own incredible volition and the support of the Aurelius Foundation prison programme.

## The Stoic lightning bolt strikes: Boris Becker's journey

Jay's story comes from one end of the socioeconomic spectrum. At the other end, there is Boris Becker – who also had a profound Stoic awakening. As mentioned, Pat Cash (1987 Wimbledon Champion) is a great supporter and believer in Stoicism. Professional athletes often come to Stoicism because it provides meaning and guidance to handle the extreme conditions of being 'in the arena', not only to survive but ultimately to thrive. Boris Becker, one of the greatest tennis players of all time, was a sensation in the late '80s and '90s – a German icon for his incredible exploits as a six-time Grand Slam Champion. These accomplishments were extraordinary but coupled with a complicated and often difficult set of choices and circumstances off the court. They culminated in Boris receiving a two-and-a-half-year custodial sentence after he was accused of, intentionally or not, deceiving creditors by hiding assets and loans after being declared bankrupt.

Boris was originally sent to HMP Wandsworth, a maximum-security prison in London, but concerns soon arose for his safety. So, Boris was transferred after a week to Huntercombe

Prison in Oxfordshire. There are falls from grace – think Mike Tyson in boxing – and this situation, albeit very different, was a similar fall from a high peak.

One day, Boris was in the prison library and noticed a group of inmates gathered around Andy Small, talking and discussing something. Boris inquired and was allowed to join the next session – his first real touchpoint with Stoicism. Boris experienced a similar epiphany to Jay, but had to answer a different question: *Who is responsible for me being here?* This question tormented Boris for days as he started to devour everything in Stoicism he could find.

Boris very quickly realized that it was his own lifetime of decisions that had landed him in prison, no matter whether those decisions had been made without malice or intent. He 'crossed the Rubicon' of personal responsibility and accountability through Stoicism. By the time Boris left Huntercombe, he was teaching other inmates about Stoicism through his life experiences and, true to his word, he has been a fantastic support to the Aurelius Foundation post-release. Boris Becker is a person of outstanding character.

## The ultimate Stoic meeting

Roll forward six months after Boris arrived at Huntercombe prison, and I witnessed one of the most surreal experiences of my life. On a cold, wet winter's day in 2022, with Boris soon to leave the UK on early release, the Aurelius Foundation worked

# FINAL REFLECTIONS

with Huntercombe Prison management to organize a special Stoic seminar behind the big green door at Huntercombe.

David Redhouse, the governor of the prison, kindly supported the event, where other governors, prisoners, guards and administrators from across the system, alongside Aurelius Foundation members, participated in a day of Stoic learning, education and transformation. After clearing security, Pat Cash and I entered the room. Boris was on the other side, talking with Andy. It was an emotional moment for both Boris and Pat. Both had lifted the Wimbledon trophy and thrilled audiences worldwide as global celebrity athletes, but here they were as human beings, sharing a moment of deep humanity and friendship.

The last time I had seen Boris was years before in Geneva at an elite business group event, drinking the finest champagne as guests of IWC, the Swiss watch company. I said hello to Boris that evening but nothing more – he was not the Boris I have grown to admire, respect and love today.

That day in Huntercombe was remarkable on every level – a stunning contrast of fate, destiny and fortune. As Seneca suggests, 'take note of fortune's habit of behaving just as she pleases'. Let's stand back and think from the big-picture perspective about these two events:

- ▶ Jay Adam, ex-prisoner, lecturing global CEOs in the seat of learning at the Academy of Athens.
- ▶ Boris Becker, global tennis megastar, lecturing to inmates in a cold, tough UK prison.

The contrasts and irony are mind-blowing in one sense, but from a Stoic's perspective, not so much.

The one unifying force, regardless of station in life, that can break through to a deep awakening and help develop a personal leadership model, is Stoicism. No matter where you sit on the totem pole of life at various times, Stoicism is relevant at every level and can be a source of salvation, deep reflection and, ultimately, personal transformation in your darkest hours. It can provide the framework to recover from life's greatest challenges and to thrive in periods of triumph and success. Its power has stood the test of time ever since Zeno started the Stoic movement on the steps of the Painted Stoa in Athens, after his world collapsed in the waters off Piraeus 2,300 years ago.

## Why is Stoicism so powerful? Because it works

Come to Stoicism as early as you can – before tragedy and before success. Ask Jay Adam or Boris Becker. Their stories are living proof of its power, and Huntercombe Prison has shown this in its most powerful form.

In closing, I heard an ex-military US Colonel in Athens put it this way: 'A thousand years from now, somewhere on a space station out on the rim of our solar system, there will be an astronaut pondering the same challenges of being human that we encounter today. Rest assured, she will be reading a copy of the *Meditations*. Why? Because this stuff is timeless – and most importantly, it works.'

# FURTHER READING

## JOHN SELLARS

> *Be careful about reading too many authors and every type of book ... You must stay with a limited number of writers and be fed by them if you mean to derive anything that will dwell reliably with you.*
>
> Seneca, *Letters* 2.2

If you have enjoyed learning about Stoic ideas and want to delve further, here are a few recommendations.

## The Roman Stoics

First and foremost are the works of the Roman Stoics. These are all highly accessible and easy to read without any background knowledge. My first recommendation would be Seneca's letters to his friend Lucilius. The best complete modern translation is *Letters on Ethics*, trans. M. Graver and A. A. Long (Chicago: The University of Chicago Press, 2015); an abridged version is available under the title *Fifty Letters of a Roman Stoic*. There are also good selections available in the Penguin Classics and Oxford World's Classics series.

Seneca's essays are also worth reading, and there are a number of good modern versions. I would recommend *Hardship and Happiness*, trans. E. Fantham *et al.* (Chicago: The University of Chicago Press, 2014), *Selected Dialogues and Consolations*, trans. P. J. Anderson (Indianapolis: Hackett, 2015), and *Dialogues and Essays*, trans. J. Davie (Oxford World's Classics, 2007) as all equally good places to start.

Probably the most popular Stoic text today is the *Meditations* of Marcus Aurelius, widely available in many recent translations. If I had to pick one, I would recommend the version by Robin

— FURTHER READING —

Waterfield (New York: Basic Books, 2021), although the Penguin Classics and Oxford World's Classics versions, among others, are also good. A. S. L. Farquharson's older Oxford translation is available in a compact hardback edition in the Macmillan Collector's Library series.

As we have seen, Epictetus is also an extremely important source of practical Stoic guidance. His *Discourses* and *Handbook* are both well worth reading, but are in some respects a bit more demanding than Seneca or Marcus for someone coming to the subject for the first time. I would recommend the recent translation by Robin Waterfield (*The Complete Works*, Chicago: The University of Chicago Press, 2022), but other translations in Oxford World's Classics and Penguin Classics are reliable. Epictetus' teacher Musonius Rufus can also now be easily read in *That One Should Disdain Hardships: The Teachings of a Roman Stoic*, trans. C. E. Lutz (New Haven: Yale University Press, 2020).

## Modern guides

Among modern practical literature, I'd begin by recommending three books, each of which takes inspiration from one of the three major Roman Stoics. David Fideler's *Breakfast with Seneca* (New York: W. W. Norton & Company, 2022), as the title suggests, takes Seneca as a guide and applies his insights to modern life in a highly readable and engaging way. Massimo Pigliucci's *How to be a Stoic* (London: Rider, 2017) takes the form of an imaginary conversation with Epictetus, drawing on his ideas but not hesitating to challenge him and suggesting ways to update Stoicism for the modern world. Donald Robertson's *How to Think Like a Roman Emperor* (New York: St. Martin's Press, 2019) is inspired by the ideas and example of Marcus Aurelius, drawing on both Marcus' brand of Stoicism and Robertson's experience as a psychotherapist.

There are many other popular books written about Stoicism in recent years. I shall mention just a few. Olympic gold medallist Mark Tuitert offers a highly practical guide to putting Stoic ideas into action in his *The Stoic Mindset: Ten Ancient Lessons for Modern Life* (London: Penguin Life, 2024). Brigid Delaney's *Reasons Not to Worry: How to be Stoic in Chaotic Times* (London: Piatkus, 2023) is an entertaining account of her experience of experimenting with living like a Stoic and what she learned from it. Tim LeBon's *365 Ways to be More Stoic* (London: John Murray, 2022) is a rich collection of bite-sized stories and advice packaged as daily reminders.

## Going deeper

If you want to dig deeper into the ancient philosophy that stands behind these ideas, in the first instance you might try Brad Inwood, *Stoicism, A Very Short Introduction* (Oxford: Oxford University Press, 2018) or John Sellars, *Stoicism*, 2nd edition (Abingdon: Routledge, 2025). All the key evidence for the earlier Athenian Stoics can be found translated in

## FURTHER READING

B. Inwood and L. P. Gerson, *The Stoics Reader* (Indianapolis: Hackett, 2008).

For a detailed study of the ideas in Marcus Aurelius' *Meditations*, you might look at John Sellars, *Marcus Aurelius* (Abingdon: Routledge, 2021) and then the chapters in John Sellars (ed.), *The Cambridge Companion to Marcus Aurelius' Meditations* (Cambridge: Cambridge University Press, 2025). Two recent biographies of Marcus Aurelius might also be of interest: Donald Robertson, *Marcus Aurelius: The Stoic Emperor* (New Haven: Yale University Press, 2024) and William Stephens, *Marcus Aurelius: Philosopher-King* (London: Reaktion Books, 2025).

# ACKNOWLEDGEMENTS

## The quest for meaning through mentorship

The journey towards greater meaning and purpose is often solitary, not because one is alone but because few engage with life's essential questions – the audience with which to discuss these questions is small within society. The journey as a CEO trying to lead a business is also very lonely at times because few understand the CEO's unique set of continual challenges. CEOs are always on!

In life in general or as a CEO in business, being bound by emotion and desire does not deliver positive long-term outcomes, because one becomes oblivious to the craft of living well or executing a clear and consistent business strategy. As a Stoic, I find solace in the pursuit of character development, especially in the wake of the many failures and mistakes I have made in my career.

I am profoundly grateful for the family, friends and incredible mentors who have supported, taught and guided me along the way. Much like Marcus Aurelius in Book 1 – 'Debts, Lessons and Influences' – of the *Meditations*, I want to acknowledge the individuals who have shaped my career and my life. My mentors have been there since day one:

**The Stead family:** Mum, Patricia, Dad, Paul, and my siblings Renee, Kristine and Jamie. Each one of them always loving, supporting and caring, with a sense of duty to ourselves, our family and society. Also, it was a very funny and witty family to grow up in. I felt no boundaries.

**Paul Nauman, Derek Burnett and Adrian Targett:** The best of friendship in my formative years, who remain just as close today. With loyal friends like these, you have the strength and support to attempt anything. They always bring me the greatest laughter. Pure joy.

**Richard Howes, Wayne Hampson and James Wadley:** Tennis coaches, but just as much leaders of young people who cultivated a belief in me that I could do something if I worked hard enough. They stimulated deeper faith in my own abilities and provided opportunity and self-belief.

**Joe Eastin:** My best friend, whose remarkable character, calmness, loyalty and street smarts always inspired and grounded me. Joe's unique ability to look at situations with such common sense goes beyond profound. Wisdom personified.

**David Eastin:** I never had a big brother, but if I did, I would hope it would be David. When the chips in life have been down, he was always there in every way – meaningfully.

## ACKNOWLEDGEMENTS

**Tom Rinehart and Bryan Collins:** Tenacious retail merchants and risk-takers who instilled in me the value of conviction.

**Maxine Clark:** The founder of Build-A-Bear, whose dynamic energy inspired my approach to high-energy leadership.

**Tom Kartsotis:** A bold entrepreneur and courageous business visionary of tremendous intensity, who gathered great people around him to realize huge company goals. I would have followed Tom anywhere.

**Richard Gundy:** An exceptional leader, whose unwavering loyalty to his team brought out everyone's best efforts. People followed him for who he was, not his title. His devotion to his family at the same time was a remarkable trait to observe. Discipline and temperance in spades.

**Don McCarthy:** The consummate businessman, whose blend of seriousness and humour exemplified the highest standards of excellence and fun.

**Alan Bean (Apollo 12 and fourth man on the Moon):** The astronaut who taught me the values of methodical focus, teamwork and impeccable integrity through exemplary action. Fantastic sense of humour as well.

**Pat Cash:** The great Wimbledon champion who showed me that life is not what you accomplish but who you become. Achieving is important, but that's something you do, not who you are. Incredible resilience.

**John Sellars and Christopher Gill:** Rare academics and the most interesting human beings, whose greater good contributions, humility, thoughtfulness and wisdom personify modern great Stoics. They set me on my own higher Stoic purpose by showing the way themselves.

**Andy Small, Jay Adam, Sukhraj Gill and Hollie Boe:** Remarkable people who, by their actions every day, demonstrate that Stoicism is alive, thriving and applicable in all walks of life. In a world searching for character, their committed Stoic values inspire me and all whom they encounter.

**Natalia Stead, my wife and companion for life:** The most special, fascinating, fun and beautiful person I've ever met. She sees the world for its reality but in a way that most do not understand. She saved me from myself through her patience and deep love. Stoic patience.

As I reflect on these people and their significant influences, I recognize that their individual characters and teachings have been incredible gifts that have equipped me to navigate so many challenges I could never have foreseen – from the brown bag incident to how to reconstruct organizations positively – while preserving my character as an aspiring Stoic in the business

## ACKNOWLEDGEMENTS

world. Their lessons remain my steadfast guides, reminding me that the journey toward developing character is an unending pursuit, one that shapes not just our own destiny but the legacies we leave behind within the businesses that we build. As Seneca stated, we are wise to surround ourselves with people of good character for our own improvement and, ultimately, our own salvation.

*Justin Stead*

---

Thanks first to Justin for his insistence that we write this book and his enthusiasm when doing it. Thanks also to our agent Melanie Michael-Greer who, quite independently, thought we should write this book and then extremely quickly found it a home with Michael O'Mara. The enthusiasm of everyone at Michael O'Mara and the speed at which they have turned our manuscript into a book have both been impressive. At the Aurelius Foundation, Hollie Boe and Sukhraj Gill have both supported us during the process in many ways.

*John Sellars*

# ENDNOTES

## Introduction

1. Quotation on the back cover of Marcus Aurelius' *Meditations*, translated by C. Scott Hicks and David V. Hicks (New York: Scribner, 2023).
2. See *New York Review of Books* 43, no. 15 (3 October 1996), 22.
3. See Frederick the Great's (anonymously published) *Oeuvres du philosophe de Sans-Souci* (1760), p. 146.
4. See Musonius Rufus, *Discourses* 8.

## Chapter 1: Meeting the Ancient Stoics

5. Seneca, *Letters* 16.3.
6. Epictetus, *Handbook* 51.
7. This is recounted in Diogenes Laertius, *Lives and Opinions of Eminent Philosophers* 7.2–3.
8. See Diogenes Laertius 7.168.

## Chapter 3: The Stoics on Control

9. See Epictetus, *Discourses* 1.2.29.

10. Our friend Donald Robertson has examined this influence, briefly in 'The Stoic Influence on Modern Psychotherapy', in J. Sellars, ed., *The Routledge Handbook of the Stoic Tradition* (Abingdon: Routledge, 2016), 374–88, and more fully in *The Philosophy of Cognitive-Behavioural Therapy* (London: Karnac, 2010).

11. Cicero does not name Antipater here, but the analogy accords with what else we know about his views and is widely attributed to him.

12. Tony Crabbe, *Busy: How to Thrive in a World of Too Much* (London: Piatkus, 2014), especially pp. 3–21.

13. See, as one example of this line of thought, *Meditations* 6.32.

14. On this point see *Meditations* 6.41.

## Chapter 5: What Is Character?

15. Chrysippus' example was a cylinder moving down a slope; see Cicero, *On Fate* 41–3.

16. This can be found in Plato's *Euthydemus* 278e-281e and is repeated by the Stoics in Diogenes Laertius, *Lives and Opinions of Eminent Philosophers* 7.101–5.

17. See Epictetus, *Discourses* 3.1.8.

## Chapter 7: Social Animals

18. Marcus Aurelius, *Meditations* 4.49.
19. See Cicero, *On Ends* 3.62.
20. This is reported in a fragment preserved by Stobaeus, and can be found in Ilaria Ramelli, *Hierocles the Stoic: Elements of Ethics, Fragments, and Excerpts* (Atlanta: Society of Biblical Literature, 2009), pp. 90–91.
21. Marcus Aurelius, *Meditations* 6.44.
22. See *New York Review of Books* 43, no. 15 (3 October 1996), 22.
23. Marcus Aurelius, *Meditations* 7.13.

## Chapter 9: Facing Challenges

24. Quoted in Vitruvius, *On Architecture* 6 Pr. 1.
25. See Emily Wilson, *Seneca: A Life* (London: Penguin, 2015), p. 62, with *Consolation to Helvia* 19.4.
26. See Seneca, *On Providence* 2.1.
27. Seneca, *On Providence* 3.3.
28. Seneca, *On Providence* 4.3.
29. Nassim Nicholas Taleb, *Antifragile: Things that Gain from Disorder* (London: Penguin, 2012).

## Chapter 10: The Journey to Become a Stoic Leader

30. The phrase *amor fati* was not used by the ancient Stoics and was coined much later by Friedrich Nietzsche, but it captures a core Stoic idea of embracing whatever happens.

## Chapter 11: Stoic Decision-Making

31. See Cicero, *On Duties* 3.50–53.
32. Cicero, *On Duties* 3.54–55.
33. In this section I draw on and adapt the useful account in Jack Visnjic's *The Invention of Duty: Stoicism as Deontology* (Leiden: Brill, 2021).
34. See Cicero, *On Duties* 3.37.
35. See Epictetus *Discourses* 2.10.

## Chapter 13: Reflecting on Time

36. Seneca, *On the Shortness of Life* 1.3.
37. Seneca, *On the Shortness of Life* 2.4.
38. Seneca, *On the Shortness of Life* 9.1.
39. Oliver Burkeman, *Four Thousand Weeks: Time Management for Mortals* (London: Vintage, 2022), p. 4, quoting the opening paragraph of *On the Shortness of Life* 1.1.

40. See https://www.who.int/data/gho/data/themes/mortality-and-global-health-estimates/ghe-life-expectancy-and-healthy-life-expectancy. These figures relate to 2021–22.

## Chapter 14: Stoic CEO Time Management

41. See Seneca, *On the Shortness of Life* 1.3–4.

## Chapter 15: The Big Picture

42. The phrase comes from the title of an essay by Pierre Hadot in his *Philosophy as a Way of Life* (Oxford: Blackwell, 1995).

43. See e.g. Marcus Aurelius, *Meditations* 4.46.

## Chapter 17: Next Steps

44. See Epictetus, *Discourses* 2.18.1–2.

45. See Epictetus, *Discourses* 2.18.5–12.

46. See Epictetus, *Discourses* 4.12.1–2.

47. Musonius Rufus fr. 52.

48. See Epictetus, *Discourses* 3.16.

49. See e.g. Cicero, *On Ends* 3.21.

# INDEX

## A

Adam, Jay 229–31, 233
Agrippa, Marcus 93
Alexander the Great 87
*amor fati* – love of fate 123–5, 126
'antifragile' 110
Antipater of Tarsus 14, 23, 42–3, 130–32, 133, 170
Antoninus Pius 18, 122, 143
Antony, Mark 144–5
Aristippus 105
Arius Didymus 93
Arrian 20
Athenodorus Cananites 93
Athens 22–3
Augustus, Emperor 93, 144–5
Aurelius, Emperor Marcus 9, 15, 17–19, 25, 27, 35, 69, 83, 85, 122, 135, 141, 145–6, 176, 205, 213, 225
  as 'CEO of the Roman corporation' 27–33
  change and impermanence 192–3
  on character 59, 69, 127, 219
  community/cosmopolitanism 88–90, 137–8
  and control 45–7, 49, 56, 168
  decision-making 143, 158
  facing challenges 106–7, 111
  interconnectedness 189–90
  on mortality and living in the present 111, 167–9, 175
  responding to dilemmas 137–8, 139
  teams and teamwork 94–7, 101
  'the view from above' 187–9, 195, 198
Aurelius Foundation 115, 215–16, 225, 226–7, 228, 232–3
Avidius Cassius 96

## B

Becker, Boris 115–16, 227, 231–3

## C

Caesar, Emperor Julius 145
Caligula, Emperor 21, 145
Caracalla, Emperor 146
Cash, Pat 115–16, 217, 227, 233
CEOs and Stoic philosophy
  *amor fati* – accept and love your fate 123–5
  importance of character 80, 81
  importance of experience 121–2

# INDEX

Stoic decision-making and accountability 147–58
Stoic-led teams/Stoic team-building 97–101
Stoic time management 173–84
taking 'the view from above' 198–203
understanding the dichotomy of control 51–6
challenges/adversity, facing 32–3
*amor fati* – accept and love your fate 123–5
in business 117–18, 121–2, 123–5
preparing for 111–12
the Stoics on 103, 104–9, 110–12, 120
*see also* dilemmas, dealing with
change and impermanence 192–3, 194
character
consistency 79, 80, 211–12, 219
development 71–3, 80
four cardinal virtues 64–8
importance in business 73–8
pursuing external success 66–7, 129–30
the Stoics on 61–8, 127, 129–30
children and Stoic education 226–7
*Chronos* and *Kairos* 174–5
Chrysippus 14, 23
Cicero 42, 86
doing the right thing 136
Case Study 1: The Grain Ship 130–32
Case Study 2: Selling Your House 132–3
downfall of 144–5, 147
civic responsibility, leadership and 32
Claudius, Emperor 21, 29
Cleanthes 14, 23
Clinton, Bill 9, 89
Commodus, Emperor 145–6
consistent behaviour 211–12, 219
control
the dichotomy of control and improved decision-making 54–6
the Stoics on 37–47, 66, 136, 168
understanding the dichotomy of control as a CEO 51–4
cosmopolitanism/global community 87–90, 137–8
courage, virtue of 10, 64, 155, 200
Covid-19 global pandemic 153–7, 200

# D

death and mortality 111, 166–7, 170, 175–6
debate and discussion, encouraging 96, 100
decision-making 10, 31, 51, 54–6, 64, 80
CEO decision-making and accountability 147–58
Cicero 143, 144–5
firing decisions 151–2, 154–5, 200

pinch points of conflicts 151–2
responding to dilemmas 130–39
Stoic decision layering process 152–7
*Dialogues* (Seneca) 21
dilemmas, dealing with 215–17
   Stage 1: Pause 134–5
   Stage 2: Is this virtuous? 136–7
   Stage 3: The right thing
      'big picture' principles 137–8
      'role' principles 138–9
Diogenes of Babylon 14, 130–32, 133
discipline in leadership 219–22
*Discourses* (Epictetus) 19–20, 41, 129, 135, 208

## E

education in Stoicism 226–33
*Elements of Ethics* (Hierocles) 15
emotional reactions 134–5
empowerment, organizational 55, 57
environmental, social, governance (ESG) strategies 32
Epictetus 15, 19–20, 22, 45, 62, 64, 115, 123, 225
   on control 37–42, 66, 136
   facing challenges 103
   on habits 207–10, 211
   responding to dilemmas 129, 135, 136, 138
ethics in business and leadership 30, 31, 44
external success, pursuing 66–7, 129–30

## F

failures/mistakes, learning from 71
Federer, Roger 149, 217
firing decisions 151–2, 154–5, 200
Fronto 94, 143

## H

habit development 62, 207–8
   avoiding negative influences 210–11
   consistency 211–12
   virtuous and vicious circles 208–9
Hadrian, Emperor 18, 143
*Handbook* (Epictetus) 20, 37, 38, 40, 41, 123
Hierocles 15, 86–7
honesty and integrity 71, 73, 76–8, 81
Huntercombe, HMP 227–8, 229–33

## I

inner citadel, building your *see* practices, daily Stoic
interconnectedness 189–92, 193

## J

justice, virtue of 10, 64, 154, 200

## L

leadership
   *amor fati* – love of fate 123–5

# INDEX

and character 62–8, 71–5
civic responsibility 32
ethics/ethical decision-making 30, 31
facing challenges/adversity 117–18, 120–23
habits and consistency 207
importance of discipline 219–22
management of resources 32
mentorship and influence 33
Musonius Rufus on 9–10
proving oneself 121–2
taking a higher perspective 187–9, 193–4, 198–203
teams/teamwork 93–101
understanding the dichotomy of control 51–7
*Letters* (Seneca) 13, 91, 120
life expectancy 166–7, 175–6
loyalty, maintaining 96, 98–9

## M

McCarthy, Don 78, 81, 181–2
mastery *vs* control 44
*Meditations* (Marcus Aurelius) 9, 15, 17, 18–19, 25, 35, 45, 46, 49, 56, 59, 69, 83, 89, 94–5, 99, 106, 127, 135, 137, 139, 141, 167, 168, 169, 188, 189, 190, 195, 205, 213, 219, 234
mental health 119, 121
mentorship and influence 33, 77–8, 241–5
moderation/temperance 10, 64, 154–5, 200
*Moral Letter* (Seneca) 22, 30
Musonius Rufus 9, 15, 20, 223

## N

*Natural Questions* (Seneca) 22
Nature and interconnectedness 189–92, 193
negativity, avoiding 208, 210–11
Nero, Emperor 15, 20, 21, 29–30, 67, 106, 145–7

## O

*On Benefits* (Seneca) 22
*On Clemency* (Seneca) 22, 67
*On Duties* (Cicero) 130
*On Ends* (Cicero) 42
*On Providence* (Seneca) 103, 108, 113
*On the Shortness of Life* (Seneca) 30, 159, 161–6, 171

## P

Panaetius of Rhodes 15, 23, 130
parental love 85–6
patience 122
perspective, taking a higher 187–94, 198–203
*Philippics* (Cicero) 144
power sharing 95, 97, 101
practices, daily Stoic 218–22
*praemeditatio futurorum malorum* 112
Praetorian Guard 95, 97
pragmatism, strategic 95, 97–8
present, living in the 167–9
prison and Stoic education 227–33

## R

rational behaviour 212
regrets 168
resilience, emotional 115–16, 125
respect, maintaining 73
retail industry and growth of e-commerce 53–4
risk analysis 32–3
risk management strategies 55

## S

self-preservation and relationships 85–6
Seneca, Lucius Annaeus 13, 15, 17, 21, 79, 91, 120, 159, 177, 235
   as 'COO of the Roman corporation' 29–33
   on facing challenges/adversity 103, 105–6, 107–9, 110, 113, 120
   flaws and downfall of 145–7
   on the value of time 161–6, 171, 175, 184
   on virtuosity 67–8
skill development 43–4
social animals, humans as 85–90, 137–8
social media, influence of 119
Socrates 22, 23, 63
stakeholders, communication with 55
stress and anxiety 54, 168

## T

Taleb, Nassim 110

teams and teamwork 94–101, 148
time, value of
   CEO time management 177–84
   concepts of *Chronos* and *Kairos* 174–5
   life expectancy 166–7
   living in the present 167–9
   ordering priorities 173–7, 184
   the Stoics on 161–70, 184

## V

value judgements 39–40, 62, 134–5
virtues, Stoic cardinal 9–10, 63–8, 80, 94, 101, 129, 154–6, 200
virtuous and vicious circles 208–9

## W

wisdom, virtue of 10, 64, 154, 200

## X

Xenophon 23

## Z

Zeno of Citium 14, 22–3, 87–8, 105, 225, 230, 234